HOW TO DO ACCENTS

Edda Sharpe

Jan Haydn Rowles

OBERON BOOKS

LONDON

First published in 2007 by Oberon Books Ltd
521 Caledonian Road, London N7 9RH
Tel: 020 7607 3637 / Fax: 020 7607 3629
e-mail: info@oberonbooks.com
www.oberonbooks.com

A catalogue record for this book is available from the British
Library.

ISBN: 1 84002 600 6 / 978 1 84002 600 9

Printed by Golden Cup Printing Co, Ltd, Hong Kong

Contents

ACKNOWLEDGEMENTS AND THANKS

For their help with the making of this book we would like to thank: Arsher Ali, Laura Caroll, Kevin Coe, Trevor Cuthbertson (also one of our test readers), Sid Dixon, Louise Dolan, Katie Draper, Joanna Gaskell, Darren Halley, Wilbur Heynes, Donna Humphries, Dylan Kennedy, Martin Larmour, David Lyons, Jor'el Mitchell (also one of our test readers), Channelle Owen, Catrin Picand-Jones, Nora Ryan Taylor, for their accent samples; Matt Walters at Quince Studios; Mariele Runacre-Temple and Gill Sharpe for the drawings and illustrations; our test readers, including Richard Ryder and Julie Legrand, for their comments and input, and Professor Valerie Hazan (Professor of Speech Science and Head of the Department of Phonetics and Linguistics, University College London) for her input and advice.

A huge thank you to all past and present students of ours, especially to those at East 15 Acting School, who have continually deepened our understanding of working with actors; to all those professional actors and directors who have fed our passion over the years; to all the staff at East 15 for your ongoing commitment to actor training; and of course to Billy's Café. (Well, you have to have your planning meetings somewhere!)

Jan would like to thank Lyn Darnley, Head of Voice at the RSC, good friend and colleague, for her support over the last 21 years, Jeanette Nelson, Head of Voice at the National Theatre, and other fellow voice teachers who have inspired and encouraged – Jane Boston, David Carey, Tess Dignan, Penny Dyer, Ailsa Gudgeon, and Christina Gutekunst – and special thanks to Cathy Weate for getting us to 'make the call'. Thanks also to friends and family for the regular 'check-ins', the listening ear and the odd glass of red, and to the Sharpe family for all their support and care. Special thanks to Siobhan for her endless encouragement and to Alex for the 'space', and of course the biggest thanks to my very dear friend, colleague and fantastic co-writer Edda: thank you for the most fun-filled, laughter-led and inspirational times. (See you next Thursday for Empire biscuits and Barry's tea.)

Edda would like to thank Jackie Maxwell, Christopher Newton and Neil Monroe, of the Shaw Festival Theatre, Canada, for their support and belief in her work over the last ten years, and Sarah Shippobotham for being the other half of a great team of two. I would also like to thank Christina Gutekunst and John Gillett not only for their friendship but also for their professional and personal integrity; my parents, for their incredible, unending belief in and support of me; my sister for always being there; Wilbur for his love, patience and good humour and for undoing all the knots, and my children, Sid and Beth, for helping me to keep it real. Of course, a very special thank you to my friend and professional soul mate, Jan. We could not have done it alone!

INTRODUCTION

How this book came about

Acting with an accent can be a dream or a nightmare for an actor. The pressures to get it right – to sound authentic, honest and connected – grow as audiences become more demanding and the world gets smaller.

Actors currently have only two options: to work with a specialist dialect coach, or to buy a specific dialect 'study tape'. In *How to Do Accents* we offer actors a new approach. Speaking with an accent is a skill just like any other: it can be learned and developed, and it is our aim with this book to provide you with the tools to do just that.

Much current accent teaching comes from the perspective of the phonetician. Actors sometimes get the feeling that before they can approach an accent they must understand the phonetic alphabet. Although this approach provides some people with a sense of security, it deals with only a small part of what makes up an accent. Moreover, the vast majority of actors find this approach at best alienating and at worst simply boring. Unfortunately this can lead them to ignore the essential structure inherent in accents, believing this leaves them free to learn on a more intuitive level. The results are accents that are extremely hit and miss to begin with, and once the actor's emotions kick in the accent flies out of the window. It simply isn't in their muscle memory, and how can it be? Intuition is essential, but so is structure. The very word 'structure' may be causing you to glaze over, but, if you think about it, it is hardly an alien concept to actors. They use it every day in their craft. They learn the structure of lines, of moves, even the structure of emotions. The structure of accents can be part of this: it simply needs to be accessible.

What is desperately needed is a simple, reassuring method for both learning and teaching accents: a method that allows the actor to use their gift for intuition in tandem with their ability to retain structure; a method that liberates the nervous while developing the skills of the keen; a method that teaches actors not just one accent, but the underlying structure inherent in *all* accents. This book provides such a method.

Using solid technical know-how, clear practical steps, real-life examples, and the occasional dose of humour, *How to Do Accents* brings to the surface the underlying structure of accents, sharing the processes that we, as specialist dialect coaches, have developed, to give you the insight, tools and confidence to work with *any* accent.

What this book is not...

This is not a linguistic or phonetic text book, but it is completely compatible with them. We have taken the language of the linguist and translated it into the language of the actor. We have distilled the very detailed work of phoneticians and extracted the elements relevant to the specific goals of the actor at work.

So who's this book for?

- The drama student
- The actor working with accents and dialect coaches
- The voice and dialect teacher
- The drama teacher
- Anyone who's ever wondered *How to Do Accents*!

What's in this book

1 **Get started** (page 17)

This chapter covers the preparation needed in order to build your new accent successfully:

- Knowing your equipment.
- Making and using a resource recording.
- Establishing the cultural context of an accent.

2 **The Foundations** (page 33)

This chapter takes you through the four essential elements needed for a solid accent *foundation*:

- **The Setting** – The setting of the muscles of the face and mouth.
- **The Zone** – Where the sound is placed.
- **The Tone** – The resonant quality of the accent.
- **The Direction** – The direction in which the voice is sent.

3 **The Two Planets** (Rhotic v Non-Rhotic) (page 47)

In this chapter you will discover that when it comes to accents the world divides into two planets:

- **Planet Rhotic**, where people say an R whenever it is written.
- **Planet Non-Rhotic**, where people only say an R if there is a vowel sound spoken after it.

More significantly you'll discover which planet you're on, and how to pass as a local on the other!

4 **The Bite** (Consonants) (page 59)

Consonants break up the flow of the voice into **Bite**-size pieces. Using diagrams and physical exercises, you will learn the '**Major Players**' to listen for in a new accent and hear the powerful effect they can have. You will also become familiar with the geography of your mouth and feel the way the voice, tongue, teeth and lips interplay in a way specific to each accent.

5 **The Shapes** (Vowels) (page 113)

The **Shapes** of vowels are at the heart of authentic accents. This chapter shows you how to establish the vowel shapes of an accent and, using visual aids and clear physical instructions, you will discover a spectrum of vowel possibilities in your own mouth.

6 The Groove (page 149)

Every accent has its own music, made up of the interplay of intonation patterns and rhythms that we call the **Groove**. In this chapter we show you how to put the cultural, historical and geographical frame around your groove, giving roots and depth to your new accent, and how to incorporate a feeling for that new groove into your voice and body. We then take you into the world of **Intonation**, refining your ability to listen to, understand, and recreate the specific intonation patterns essential to communication.

7 Get Professional (page 171)

In this chapter we show you how to take your accent into the professional arena and onto a professional level. This means knowing not just how to *do* an accent, but also how to keep on improving it and how to work with it in different professional contexts: within a production, in relation to the director, the rehearsals and the character itself, and getting it ready for auditions and sight-reading.

How to use this book

Ever wondered why you're great at doing West Midlands but stray far and wide when attempting a Newcastle accent? Maybe you have a great instinct for tune, but you're not noticing consonants. Or maybe you have a great ear for rhythm, but you haven't noticed vowel shapes. Recognising patterns, knowing the limited options available to your accent and having a simple structure for remembering them are all key to being able to do an accent.

Being good at accents is about so much more than 'having a good ear'. It is about using *all* your available senses to learn new skills, just as you did as a small child. For this reason we encourage you throughout the book to **see**, **feel** and **hear** new accents.

When you were a child you dedicated hours to hearing the sounds, and/ or seeing the shapes of the faces around you, playing with the shape of your mouth, until the sounds and shapes *you* were making matched the sounds and shapes you were *hearing* and/or *seeing*. Then you practised those shapes and movements over and over again until they became locked into your muscle memory. That's what children do. That's what you did and how you learned to speak. That's why you have an accent, even if you think you don't!

For some of you, your mimicry instinct may still be active – maybe you've always enjoyed playing with new sounds – while others of you may have turned it off long ago, happy to sound like those around you. Whichever you are, prepare to switch your mimicry instinct back on and practise as hard as a child!

You can use this book to learn a specific accent or to learn the structure inherent in all accents, using your own resource material and/or the CD provided. You may want to work through the book systematically, working step by step through the different elements. Or perhaps you are someone who likes to dip in and out of books when the need arises, picking out the relevant bits and getting a good overview. Either way this book will work for you.

We have broken the architecture of accents into five areas: **The Foundations**; **The Two Planets**; **The Bite**; **The Shape**; and **The Groove**. These define the principal points of change from one accent to another. By necessity we have used a limited selection of accents as our examples, but the patterns demonstrated will apply to any accent.

If you are using *How to Do Accents* as a work book to develop your understanding of how accents work, or if you are building up the profile of a specific accent, it is best to take one area of the work at a time. Give your brain time to absorb new information and to get used to the new way of interpreting and creating sound. Working steadily for half an hour or so a day can be better than doing two solid hours once a week. Where possible, find the pace that works for you.

Through the book you will see these icons:

See It

 This icon prompts you to concentrate in a visual way, either by looking at an illustration, using your mind's eye, or looking in a mirror.

Feel It

 This icon prompts you to focus on physical processes and feelings.

Hear It

There are two **Hear It** icons:

 This icon prompts you to listen to a track on the accompanying CD…

 …while this icon prompts you to listen to yourself.

When learning new sounds it helps to have a way of listening to yourself that is instant and gives you an accurate 'outside ear' on the sounds you are making. You can do this by 'funnelling' the sound from your mouth straight back to your ear.

Creating your funnel

Put one hand about five centimetres (two inches) away from your mouth, cup it onto the bottom of the other hand which then in turn cups behind the ear, creating a funnel from one to the other:

You will know you've got the position right when you hear your voice loud and clear, even when you are speaking quietly. This is especially invaluable when you are working in a group, or when you need to practise quietly.

Remember, learning how to do accents is just like anything else you've successfully learnt: riding a bike, speaking a language, or even navigating a new mobile phone. To begin with, you separate out the different elements, identify what you know, recognise what you don't know and then learn, re-learn and practise. During this process your awareness is very high and the focus and juggling can seem complicated. Some things seem to come easily; others seem to take longer to get into the muscle memory. Don't worry – this just means there is more learning taking place! Soon, and with practice, the elements come together and the process seems natural and effortless.

The important thing is not to overwhelm your brain. Learning an accent is all about layering. Take it a piece at a time, practise all the pieces and then

HOW TO DO ACCENTS

put them all together. And above all be prepared to make mistakes and sound silly: this is just you and your brain learning!

You and the New

One thing that will really help you to do *other* accents is understanding your *own*. By building a profile of the qualities specific to your own accent you can establish a solid base from which to navigate other accents.

If you look towards the back of the book (pages 187–95), you will see a chart called **You and the New**. You will be prompted at the end of each chapter to fill it in. Once filled in, this will provide you with an instant comparison between your accent and the new accents you are working on, showing you where the most significant changes are. Photocopy this before you start, as you may want to use it each time you learn a new accent. (Alternatively, you can download the chart as a ready-to-print pdf from the *How to Do Accents* website at **www.howtodoaccents.com**.)

1

GET STARTED

IN THIS CHAPTER...

We introduce you to three areas that you need to be on top of before you begin work on any accent:

1 **Knowing your equipment.** Accents are physical. They are made by your body. In order to adapt you will need to have some basic knowledge of the physical equipment you have and how it works. In this section we introduce you to those basics.

2 **Making and using a Resource Recording.** One essential practical requirement when learning a new accent is a resource recording. You cannot learn an accent out of thin air. In this section we show you how to find, make and use a resource recording to get the most from yourself and this book!

3 **Getting into the Scene.** Accents don't exist in a vacuum. They are made by living, breathing communities, subject to the vagaries of history, politics, peer pressure, climate, culture, economics and more. You name it: somewhere along the line external influences have had and continue to have an effect on the way we speak. Contextualising your accent is a vital step towards owning it and making it real.

Knowing your equipment

Our lips, jaw, tongue, soft palate and cheeks are always on the move, flicking, tapping, gliding and making contact with one another, dancing their way through thousands and thousands of different shapes and sounds, and yet we don't give it a second thought!

In order to understand how all these shapes and sounds are made you will need to become familiar with your own bits, the **Articulators**. You will need to know what the various parts are called, which part is being used, and how the various parts make contact.

In other words, to do accents you will need to know which *active* articulator is doing what with which *passive* articulator!

It may be that you already have a good understanding of all this, but if this is all new to you, or you feel in need of a refresher, read on.

Throughout this book we will be using this simplified diagram of the articulators:

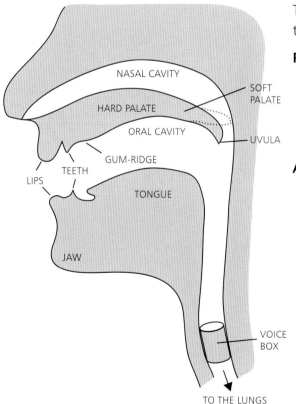

The articulators divide into two groups:

Passive (non-moving)

1   Teeth

2   Upper gum-ridge

3   Hard palate

Active (moving)

1   Lips/cheeks

2   (Lower) Jaw

3   Tongue

4   Soft palate

See It and Feel It

You will need a mirror so you can see what we are talking about!

The non-movable or **Passive articulators** are the ones you're just stuck with (unless you have surgery…). Using your tongue, explore the *passive* articulators and connect what you feel to the diagram.

It is the passive articulators that provide the structures against which the **Active articulators** play. The *active* articulators are the ones that do all the work.

Using the mirror, explore your *active* articulators:

1 LIPS and CHEEKS:

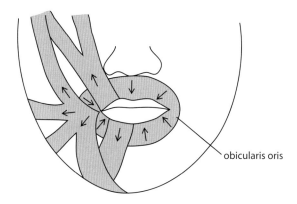

obicularis oris

The muscles of the lips and cheeks are interconnected.

Your **lips** have one principal muscle called the *obicularis oris*. This muscle divides into *inner* and *outer sphincter* actions. When you use the outer sphincter your lips can round like this:

and when you use the inner sphincter they round like this:

Some accents prefer one of these actions above another. Some like to make a proper circle, using a lot of rounding, while some use almost no rounding at all. Your **cheeks** have three principal muscle groups which pull the mouth in various directions:

- **sideways** into smiles, grins, etc
- **downwards** into a grimace
- **upwards** into sneers.

Try making these faces to see and feel these muscles at work. One or other of these muscles may be habitually loose or tight, active or passive in an accent.

2 JAW:

The lower jaw is attached to the upper jaw by muscle and ligament. To find this muscle, clench your teeth as if you are biting something with your back teeth. As you do this, put your fingers on your cheeks, just in front of your ears. You will feel the jaw muscle (the masseter) bunching. Try to picture how much space you have between your top and bottom teeth at the back as you sit at rest. The larger the space (without pulling), the looser the muscle. The jaw muscle holds different degrees of tension and looseness in different individuals and different accents.

3 TONGUE:

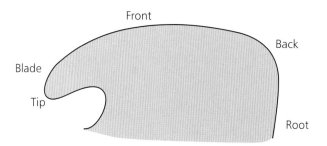

The tongue is a surprisingly large organ. It is probably bigger than you think. It often surprises people that the entire body of muscle, right down to the underside of the chin, is in fact your tongue. Feel under your chin with your thumb while you push your tongue up against the roof of your mouth. What you feel pushing down against your thumb is your tongue! Look at your tongue in the mirror.
It's a bit like a separate creature living in your mouth. In fact, it is probably the most flexible and sensitive muscle in the human body. Look in the mirror to see the different sections of your tongue. To begin with, notice that your tongue divides into two main sections: a 'free' section and an 'attached' section. Look under the tongue and you will see the bit where it attaches to the jaw. This free section is the most flexible bit and is sub-divided into the **Tip** and the **Blade**. This tends to be the bit of the tongue we are most aware of. The attached section is the bit you probably overlook. This part of the tongue is sub-divided into the **Front, Centre, Back** and **Root**. The tongue will have areas of tension and looseness developed through the habitual movements of the language and accent it makes.

HOW TO DO ACCENTS

4 SOFT PALATE:

If the front of your tongue is super-flexible, you can feel your way back along the roof of your mouth, curling your tongue back on itself until you feel a ridge. That is the end of the hard palate and the beginning of the soft palate. Get a mirror, and look at the little punch bag that dangles in the back of your mouth (you'll need to get the light in the right place to see inside). That's your **Uvula**. It hangs from the very end of the soft palate. (You can stun someone at a party with that piece of information!) The job of the soft palate is to direct the breath or voice into either the nose or the mouth. In some accents, such as Manchester and Essex, the soft palate is held low, giving the sound a lot of 'nasal spill'; in some, such as West Ireland and North Yorkshire it is high, creating a more oral sound; while in others, such as Standard English (RP), it has to bounce gymnastically up and down. Look again at the picture on page 19 and you will see how it can open or close the passage to the nose. So you can see that having a flexible soft palate is essential in order to do accents.

- To see the soft palate *lift up* and close the passageway to your *nose*, make a yawn while keeping your tongue flat and forward in your mouth. You'll see the little punch bag shoot up and disappear. Make an 'AH' as you do this and feel the sound resonating in the mouth.
- To see it *drop down* and close the passageway to your *mouth*, open your mouth and say 'NG', the sound from the end of the

word **sing**. You will see the back of the tongue and the soft palate come together and feel the sound resonating in the nose.

- To feel it *bounce* switch from the closed 'NG' to the yawned 'AH' in one action. If your soft palate is a bit sluggish, the 'AH' will end up in your nose! See if you can switch the direction of sound from your nose to your mouth. You may need to give it a bit of exercise to tone up that muscle!

So those are your **articulators**. But of course, they only form speech when they have something to play with, and that's where your voice box comes in…

5 VOICE BOX:

As the air leaves your lungs it passes through a piece of equipment called your **voice box** (also called the **larynx**). This 'box' contains two folds of flesh (**vocal folds**) that can either stay open to let air pass through unimpeded, or come together so that the outgoing air produces vibrations as it moves through them. You can see the voice box in the front of your neck. It's what a lot of us call the 'Adam's Apple'. Put your fingers on your neck and swallow and you will feel it bounce up and down. Men's voice-boxes are generally larger than women's and consequently they make lower notes.

To feel your voice vibrations 'switching on and off' try the following:

- Make a long 'V' and, without stopping the air flow, change it to an 'F'. You will feel the voice switch off.

HOW TO DO ACCENTS

- Reverse this: start with an 'F' and change it to a 'V'. You will feel the voice switch on.
- On one breath change from 'F' to 'V' a number of times. You will feel the voice switching on and off as the folds come together then apart, together, then apart.

You can do the same thing with an 'S' and 'Z' too. If you feel your face, neck and chest as you make voice vibrations you can feel the vibrations resonating. Speech sounds are made with both breath and voice vibrations. (You will often see this distinction described as 'voiced' and 'voiceless'.) Your articulators play with the air and vibrations in your mouth, holding them, diverting them, and shaping them to create the specific speech sounds of your language and accent.

So that's your bits!

Of course, the really clever thing is the way we move them about and bring them together. Make an 'FF' sound and you'll feel your top teeth contact your bottom lip. Add voice vibrations to this shape and the sound changes to a 'V'. Make a 'K' and you're feeling the back of the tongue lift up to contact the soft palate. Add voice vibrations and you're making a 'G'.

With all these moving parts, awareness and flexibility are the key to doing accents. This book will increase your flexibility as you explore new ways of playing with the sounds in your mouth. If you want to improve your basic voice use then it may help to invest in a good voice book such as *Finding Your Voice* by Barbara Houseman, or *The Voice Book* by Michael McCallion. (See 'Recommended Reading' in the Appendix, page 221.)

Working with a resource recording

In order to have something to mimic it is essential to have a good **resource recording**: a recorded example of at least one real speaker speaking in the accent you are looking to learn. (After all, children don't learn to speak in a vacuum!)

It's amazing the number of actors we meet who say, 'I've tried to do a Welsh accent (or Irish, or Newcastle, etc) and I'm rubbish!' – only to discover the only time they've ever actually *heard* it was when they went there on holiday ten years before. People have such high expectations of their poor old brains: they seem to expect to be able to do an accent without giving their eyes, ears and mouths a chance to really absorb and learn it. Give yourself a break. You could be brilliant if you had the right tools and practised in the right way!

Here's what you will need:

1   A good resource recording – as we have already said, this is a recorded example of real speakers (at least one and preferably more) using the accent you wish to learn. This is absolutely *essential*.

2   This book. (Obviously.)

3   A mirror.

4   Something to record yourself on that can also play back. (Possibilities include a cassette tape recorder, a MiniDisc recorder, a computer with a sound card, a dictation machine. Most of these will need a separate microphone. Many digital cameras also have an audio recording facility.)

5   Paper and pencil to make any notes.

The CD that comes with this book has resource recordings of 11 accents of English. You can find them on Tracks 86–96 on the CD. They are:

- *Standard American* (TRACK 86)
- *Northern Ireland/Belfast* (TRACK 87)
- *Southern Ireland/Cork* (TRACK 88)
- *Scottish/Glasgow* (TRACK 89)
- *Newcastle-upon-Tyne* (TRACK 90)
- *Manchester* (TRACK 91)
- *Liverpool* (TRACK 92)
- *South Wales/Swansea* (TRACK 93)
- *West Midlands/Walsall* (TRACK 94)
- *East End of London* (Two voices: *Cockney* and *Contemporary London*) (TRACK 95)
- *Standard English (RP)* (TRACK 96)

If you want to learn a different accent from these you will need your own resource recording, and here's how to get one…

Making your own resource recording

The best way of getting what you want is to do it yourself. Here's how:

- Find a willing candidate or candidates to record. Two examples are better than one, as you will then have more information to work from.

HOW TO DO ACCENTS

It can also help to have a conversation between two people with the same accent, as their accents will feed off each other. Try places like cultural centres, universities, acting schools, embassies and tourist centres to find the people you want. Remember to be as specific about age, gender, cultural background, etc, as you can: these things can make a huge difference.

- Here's what you will need:

  - a portable recording device (it doesn't matter how up to date it is so long as it works!)

  - the KIT LIST (see Appendix, page 206)

  - Major Player Elicitation sentences (see Appendix, page 207)

  - the Standard Text (see Appendix, page 208)

  - questions to elicit conversational speech (see below and Appendix, page 207).

Top Tips for recording people

Practise using your recording device: it really doesn't help someone to be at their ease if you fumble about with microphones.

This may be obvious but…do a test to make sure it's recording! (Jan has several old dialect tapes with nothing on them because her pause button was still on.)

Make sure the device is next to *them* and not you. You want their voice, not your own! (Edda has many a tape from her early days where she is loud and clear and the person being interviewed can be heard faintly in the distance.)

When eliciting conversational speech, it is important to get people to talk easily in an animated way. It can also be the hardest thing to get from some people. How often have we listened to someone regale us with stories, only to have them clam up the minute they see a microphone! Remember, you are trying to get a good source of genuine speech patterns. In this section of recording you want to get a good example of the changes in pace and music use that happen as meanings and feelings change. These are some suggestions of questions that can often get good results. Take them with you to have ready prompts for the conversation.

- What food do you most miss from home?
- What is the scenery like in your area?
- What's your ideal home?
- What music do you like/dislike?
- What qualities do you value in a friendship?
- What 'bad habits' do you dislike in a person?
- How do you think your accent is perceived by others?
- What was your favourite childhood game/toy?

Where to find existing resource recordings

It is possible to find good commercial recordings, though they more than likely don't have the KIT LIST or Standard Text in them. There are plenty of helpful booklets with CDs on the market (Allyn Partin and Gillian Lane Plescia, for example, produce a wealth of good recordings with basic vowel information and native speakers) and this book will enable you to use those materials more successfully.

Needless to say, the internet is an invaluable resource. With good broadband facilities you can hear the sounds of the world, and, where copyright allows, even burn them onto your own CDs. We have given a list of some of the websites that we have found most useful in the Appendix (page 209).

Another handy resource can sometimes be films which have specific geographic settings – think *Brassed Off* (West Yorkshire), *The Full Monty* (South Yorkshire), *Midnight in the Garden of Good and Evil* (Savannah, Georgia), *The Field* (rural Southern Ireland), *In the Name of the Father* (Belfast), etc – not least because you get good visual information. But be careful: although they can be great for getting a general flavour of the sounds of the area, the actors may or may not be doing a genuine local accent!

How to listen to your resource recording

Once you have found or made your recording there are ways and means of listening to it to get the best out of both it and you.

Unstructured listening

To begin with, let yourself respond intuitively to get your juices flowing! You may well find yourself wanting to mimic immediately, so do. Always remember to encourage that instinct. Write down anything – and we mean *anything* – you notice: perhaps the tune strikes you first, maybe it sounds 'flat', or a bit 'choppy'; or perhaps you notice specific words, either because they are unusual words or because they say them in a very different way from you. You'll probably find you are noticing a lot in this unstructured way. As you work through this book you will be able to put these initial discoveries into the structure of your new accent.

If you have a video or DVD recording you can also look at the shapes the speakers are making, how the mouth is held, how much the jaw, lips and cheeks move, or don't. These are all things worth noticing.

Structured listening

Unstructured listening only kick-starts the process. What this book will show you is the next vital step: how to listen in a *structured* way.

As you work through this book we will give you examples of specific sounds and combinations of sounds on the CD that accompanies the book. These are the sounds to listen for on your resource recording. You will probably need to listen to the same phrase on your resource recording many times over for your ear to identify the element you are listening for, both for your mouth to accurately mimic it, and for your brain to retain it. (Once simply won't be enough!)

Get into the scene

Accents don't exist in a vacuum. They are made by living, breathing communities, subject to the vagaries of history, politics, peer pressure, climate, culture, economics and more. Contextualising your accent is a vital step towards owning it and making it real. Remember, as the world gets smaller, authenticity becomes ever more important.

Putting it into a cultural and physical context

- It sounds obvious, but know where you are on the map! Everywhere exists in relation to somewhere else: you have to know your neighbours to know yourself (one of those clichés that happens to be true). When you see how close they are on the map it's hardly surprising that when you do a Newcastle accent you can sometimes sound Scottish. It can even be reassuring.

- Find out as much as you can about the music, dance, art and culture of an area. These influences may directly affect or indeed reflect the way people speak. Either way, immersing yourself in them helps you to feel the heartbeat of the people: think of Irish dancing and the rhythms of the bodhran; Country and Western songs bending the notes on the sliding guitar; Yiddish kletzmer music with its minor keys, fast trills and sliding notes (to name just a few significant examples).

- If you possibly can, visit the area. Nothing compares with being immersed in the accent, meeting the people and breathing in the landscape. If you can't get there, many organisations produce websites and tourist videos which can give you a flavour of the same experience.

- You may find cultural centres, organisations and community groups in your own area that have the accent you are looking for – for example, the London Welsh Centre or the New York Irish Centre. Visit them!

- We have to give a mention to the Wikipedia website. It is an incredible resource for geographical, historical, cultural and even linguistic, phonetic and phonological information on communities and their dialects.

Putting it into historical context

- Accents change over time. Influences come and go and it is important to know the period of the play you are doing and how your character fits into the social mix of the time. The accents in much of London today bear little or no relation to the accents of 50 years ago. Today in the early days of the 21st Century some young people of London have an accent heavily influenced by the sounds of African, Jamaican and Bengali, whereas the influences in the early 20th Century were French, Irish and Jewish. New accents appear with the arrival of another wave of incomers: accents such as Arabic/Chicago or Bengali/Bradford. We can't always be totally historically accurate, but knowing where your accent comes from and even where it's going will enable you to make informed choices about what to do and how to do it.

- Where you can, find a sample speaker from the right period for the play/character you are doing. It may take a bit of searching through historical sound archives. A 50-year-old speaker recorded in 1920 is giving you a window into an accent that reaches back to the 1870s. It would be inappropriate to use the accent of a present-day 17-year-old for plays such as *The Bright and Bold Design* (1930s Stoke on Trent), *Men Should Weep* (1930s Glasgow) or *The Accrington Pals* (First World War Accrington).

2

THE FOUNDATIONS

IN THIS CHAPTER...

You will learn how to build the **Foundations** of an accent. Solid foundations hold the whole structure of the accent in place.

When asked what makes one accent different from another, most people will point to differences in tune (what we will call the 'groove', page 149), two or three vowels (the 'shapes', page 113), and maybe one or two consonants (the 'bite', page 59). These are all valid important observations, but underpinning all of these are the foundations on which the groove, shapes and bite sit.

> One day we were sharing our stories of how we each discovered that we had a passion for sounds and accents. When Jan was young, she and her friend Julie Brown used to pretend they were French. This didn't involve any French language, just gobbledygook using a generally 'French' sound. They also pretended to be the 'Fonz' doing an American accent, and Lisa Goddard in Skippy doing an Australian accent. At the tender age of ten, Jan taught Julie what the difference was between those accents, explaining that:
>
> - 'American' was in the back of the mouth.
> - 'French' needed to have a particular tone to it.
> - 'Australian' was similar to 'London', but you needed to smile and grit your teeth.
>
> Contained within these apparently naïve early descriptions are the first three of the four building blocks that are the foundations of an accent.

To establish solid accent foundations, you will need these three elements to be firmly in place:

- **The Zone** – Where the sound is placed.
- **The Tone** – The resonant quality of the accent.
- **The Setting** – The setting of the muscles of the face and mouth.

With these in place, and because the voice is not a static building, you will need one more element...

- **The Direction** – The direction in which the voice is sent.

Without these foundations your accent will be unfocused and difficult to sustain, but with all four elements working together you create the solid foundations on which the rest of the accent is built.

So before we go any further let's learn how to:

- Focus the voice in a specific **Zone**.
- Hear and create a specific **Tone**.
- Feel and sustain a specific **Setting**.
- Send the voice in the right **Direction**.

...and thereby build your **Foundations**.

The Zone

Each accent has a resonant focal point, or 'placement', in the mouth that we call a **Zone**.

Small changes in the shaping of the throat and mouth, tongue and soft palate affect which zone the voice resonates in. These changes are very small, and the muscles do not respond easily to direct instructions. They are programmed as 'mimicry' muscles, and from an early age we all use them to learn how to recreate the sounds we hear around us. We can get these muscles to move again by mimicking sounds. Be bold: dive into copying the sounds in this section and wake up your basic childhood skills of mimicry. Do this consciously and notice the results you get. This will increase your skill at zoning. Notice how the voice feels in the mouth and where you feel it is focused.

In order to focus your voice into the specific zone for your accent, it helps to have a good visual image of the inside of your mouth and to picture the different zones you are aiming for. To this end we have mapped out the mouth and divided it into zones which we have numbered. At this point it will really help you to have a solid knowledge of the geography of the inside of your mouth. If you are unsure of what's what in there, go back and work through 'Knowing your equipment' (pages 19–25).

As you can see in the illustration below there are seven zones.

These zones are focused on the following areas:

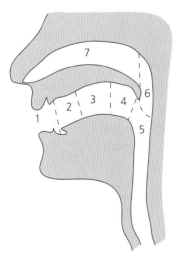

Zone 1: The **Teeth and lips**

Zone 2: The **Gum-ridge**

Zone 3: The **Hard palate**

Zone 4: The **Soft palate** and **uvula**

Zone 5: Down into the **Pharynx** (throat)

Zone 6: Up into the **Naso-pharynx** (behind the nose)

Zone 7: The **Nasal cavity** (right inside and down the nose)

When you focus your voice into each of these zones, the quality of the sound will change.

Hear It [TRACK 1]

- In order to isolate the effect of changing the zone, listen to the way Edda focused one accent – Standard English (RP) – into each of the seven zones.
- Then listen to Jan as she tunes in and finds different accents lurking in each zone.

Notice the way we 'tune in' to the zone and then keep the voice in that zone, counting on *one note*. By staying on one note you can hear that it is the *resonance* that changes from zone to zone, and not the actual pitch of the voice. Shifting the focus of the voice to a different zone may *sound* as if we are changing the pitch, but in fact it is the resonant balance of the note that is altered, giving each zone a different quality of sound.

Listen to us a few times and then have a go yourself in your own accent if you can, or simply copy what you hear.

Pick a comfortable note of your own to use and stick to it. You can reverse the order if you find it easier. Sometimes the zones at the back of the mouth are easier to feel, as the vibrations are creating stronger sensations.

You may find it hard not to change accent: each zone may bring a different accent to your mouth. That's the power of zoning!

See It

Visualise your voice as you speak with us. See it travelling and hitting the specific target point in each zone. Do this a few times to get a good sense of what you're doing. Remember you are flexing those mimicry muscles and using your mind's eye! The more you do it, the better you'll get.

Feel It

Feel the vibrations hitting the target points in each zone.

1 **Teeth and lips:** Aim the voice onto the teeth and lips and into the open space beyond! This time you may not feel the vibrations very strongly as you are aiming right through and out of the mouth with the voice touching nothing else on the way.

2 **Gum-ridge:** Aim the voice forward onto the gum-ridge. Feel the full effect of the vibrations in this area. Vibrations also pass through the gum-ridge and upper lip and vibrate in the nostrils.

HOW TO DO ACCENTS

3 **Hard palate:** Aim the voice straight up into the roof of the mouth. Feel the vibrations driving up onto the hard palate and *through the bone.*

4 **Soft palate and uvula:** Aim the voice onto the soft palate and uvula. Feel this soft tissue vibrating.

5 **Pharynx:** Aim the voice to the back of the mouth in the space behind the tongue. (You may need to think of a yawn to create more space.)

6 **Naso-pharynx:** Aim the voice behind the soft palate, keep those vibrations at the back of the nose, not down it.

7 **Nasal cavity:** Aim the voice right down the nose, and only the nose, and feel it vibrating.

Some of the zones may be easier for you to feel and hear than others. Keep working on seeing, hearing, and feeling them to really develop sensitivity and flexibility.

TOP TIP

*As the voice moves in the mouth you may **think** it sounds higher at the front and lower at the back. Don't be tempted to change the **pitch**: let the zone do the work!*

The Tone

The second essential element in building the foundations of an accent is the ability to identify and *sustain* its specific **tone**.

Ever stop talking and think you can still hear the *sound* of your voice? Or maybe someone else stopped talking and you could still hear the sound of *their* voice? Listen to a person speak for a while, don't listen to the words, but just listen to the *tone* of their voice. You can hear a tonal drone that underpins the voice no matter where the music or pitch may travel. Think of the way bagpipes sound, with the constant drone underneath the complex melody: that's the kind of thing we mean.

Every accent has a tone of its own, and when you listen to all the examples on this CD you can hear how different tones can be. Just as with the zone, the tone is created by small changes in the shaping of the throat and mouth, tongue and soft palate. The effect can be to give a sound greater depth or make it more lightweight; it may seem 'harsher' or 'softer'. Think of the twang of Tennessee or the soft airy sound of upper-class Georgia. Think about how the Queen sounds, or David Beckham. We might use words such as 'thin' or 'tight' to describe the Queen's sound. We might use words such as 'light' and 'sweet' to describe David Beckham's. We use words like this all the time to describe voices: brassy, throaty, nasal, plummy, hoarse, squeaky, boomy, whiney, etc… It is not the *pronunciation* of words we are describing here, but rather the *tone* of the voice, the quality of the sound – in fact the balance of the tonal frequencies.

Hear It [TRACK 2]

- Listen to the three speakers on the CD. Listen not to *what* they say, but only to the *tone* of their voices, the noise their voices make. (You can hear us in the background making this clearer!)

  Manchester   Cockney   Standard English (RP)
- Listen to the way we identify and tune in to the tone of each, and then sustain that tone as we count to ten.

Hear It

Now get those mimicry muscles working. Have a go yourself. Match your tone to the *tonal quality* of the speakers.

Feel It

Of course, the zone and the tone are intrinsically connected: you can't get one without the other! Identify which zone you feel the tone vibrating in. Feel the tone resonating in that zone.

See It

Visualise the tone resonating in the specific zone you have identified.

Have a go with our other sample speakers (TRACKS 86–96) in this way in order to really exercise your zoning and toning skills. Don't try to be subtle. Really try to mimic what you hear. Be playful and have fun.

HOW TO DO ACCENTS

The Setting

By layering the tone and zone together you are creating anchors for the foundations of the accent in your mouth. In order to change the zone and the tone and create the sound you want, you have to change the position and shape of your tongue, the space in your mouth, the position of the soft palate, the shape of your lips and the amount of tension in your jaw. You are changing your **Setting**.

We were laughing as we wrote this section, because we remembered a game that we play when we're on the tube. We watch people in the next carriage and try to guess their accents simply by watching their faces as they speak. Even though we can't hear them, we are able to see some of the muscular settings of the face and mouth that contribute to the sound. Jan's mum, who is not famed for her ability to do accents or impressions, gets one bit spot on: when recreating a speaker she will always pull a slightly bizarre face! What she recognises is that the speaker is using a different muscular setting from her own. Fortunately (perhaps) she doesn't have to walk on stage and recreate an accent, so her work can stop there; but if she did, this would be a very useful starting point.

Remember the active articulators we looked at in 'Knowing your equipment' (page 19–24)? They are the **cheeks**, the **lips**, the **jaw**, the **tongue** and the **soft palate**. These are the movable parts of your speech system, and all of these are involved in creating a **setting**. Your own articulators are held in their particular setting for your own accent and in order to do another accent they will have to find a new setting.

In each accent the muscles of the face and mouth are shaped and held in a particular position. After all, if your mouth has to make the same set of moves over and over again it is bound to take up a position that makes those moves possible. In Arabic, for example, the root of the tongue is tense, ready to make those guttural sounds; in Indian the tongue tip is curled up and back for the retroflexed consonants; in Canadian the body of the tongue is bunched up, ready for those R's; and so on…

When we worked with an Australian actress (who did have to walk on stage), she said that in order to get into the English accent she had to relax her cheek muscles, get a 'scooped-out' feeling in the cheeks, and make a gap between her top and bottom back teeth. These three small *adjustments made a huge difference to her **setting**, and through this setting she was more able to find and keep the zone and tone.*

Feel It, Hear It and See It

Feel your muscles being held in different settings from the ones they're used to while you count to ten, or speak the days of the week. Focus on maintaining the setting, letting that inform the sound. We've gone through the articulators one at a time so that you can really focus on the effect changes in each of them can have.

Listen to the way the quality of the sound changes with each setting.

Look at the changes in the mirror.

Cheeks:
- Let the cheeks hang loose.
- Scoop the cheeks inwards.
- Widen the cheeks in a half smile.

Lips:
- Tighten the inner muscle of the lips ('cat's bottom'!).
- Stretch the lips out into a thin, wide line.
- Pout with fat lips.

Jaw:
- Clench the teeth.
- Bounce the jaw open for the vowels.
- Drop and hold the jaw loosely open.

Tongue:
- Squeeze the tongue up and forward in a strong 'EE' position.
- Relax the tongue and let it feel fat in the mouth.
- Hold the back of the tongue high up in the mouth, as if about to do a 'G'.

Soft palate:
- Hold a yawn at the back of your mouth.
- Let the soft palate become heavy, squashing the space at the back of the mouth, like almost saying 'NG'.

Now listen to us as we describe the settings of three accents as we speak in them:

HOW TO DO ACCENTS

Hear It [TRACK 3]

- *Yorkshire*
  Cheeks: Loose
  Lips: Slack
  Jaw: Dropped
  Tongue: Heavy and flat
  Soft Palate: High

- *Scottish*
  Cheeks: Soft
  Lips: Pouted and held small
  Jaw: Mid-open
  Tongue: Rolled forward and gripped
  Soft Palate: Low

- *London*
  Cheeks: Held
  Lips: Flat (corners pinched)
  Jaw: Close
  Soft Palate: Low

So how do you identify what the setting of a particular accent is? Well, it really is a circular process: get the tone and zone and you have the setting; get the setting and you have the tone and zone. If you can see a speaker then you will get some visual clues, and when you listen to a speaker your own muscles may well find the setting for you through a sort of sympathetic response; but if you're still not sure, the biggest clue is to be found in one of the smallest sounds the speaker makes…

The Hesitation sound

The hesitation sound 'um' or 'uh', that you hear when speakers are thinking of what to say next, is the sound that is made when the mouth relaxes into in its own neutral setting.

By listening for and recreating this sound you can often identify the setting of an accent, especially if it is very different from your own!

Hear It [TRACK 4]

Listen to all these hesitation sounds… You can hear how different they can be from one accent to another!

Feel It

Copy the hesitation sounds and feel the shapes you have to make to get each sound right.

Freeze mid-sound and notice the position your muscles are in. This can give you the neutral setting for that accent.

See It

Do the above exercise, and this time look in the mirror to see how your face changes from one accent to another.

Finding and keeping the setting is *crucial*. It enables you to sustain your accent and gives it authenticity. What is most significant, and often surprising to realise, is that the settings you have to hold to make these sounds are the relaxed *effortless* settings of those speakers. When they stop speaking it is those settings that their muscles fall back into.

> **TOP TIP** ─────────────────────────────────
>
> *Make sure you relax back into the setting of the **accent** between phrases of speech, and not your **own** setting. The accent is still there in the setting of your muscles, even when you are not speaking!*

The Direction

One more thing…

…by layering the **Zone**, **Tone** and **Setting** together you have established the essential foundations of an accent, but to make it come alive you need one more thing: a direction in which to send it. Not sure what we mean? When working on any accents think about the way in which the sound seems to travel out of the mouth: it may be quite different from your own accent. When you listen to different accents you can imagine seeing the sound travelling around and out of the mouth in different directions, like arrows. It could be travelling forwards, backwards or even sideways. Listen to these examples to hear what we mean.

 ### *Hear It* (TRACKS 89–92, 95–96)

- *London*: Forward onto hard palate and teeth (95).
- *Liverpool*: Spilling sideways (92).
- *Manchester*: Held at the back, circling (91).
- *Newcastle*: Lurching back and forth (90).
- *Glasgow*: Falling back (89).
- *Standard English (RP)*: Forward and out like a wave (96).

HOW TO DO ACCENTS

See It

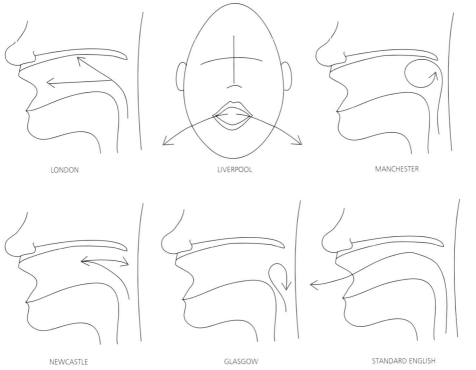

LONDON   LIVERPOOL   MANCHESTER

NEWCASTLE   GLASGOW   STANDARD ENGLISH

Feel It

Using the KIT LIST or Set Text, have a go at any of these accents and send your voice in the described direction and you will notice what an effect it has!

Putting it all together

Zone, **Tone**, **Setting** and **Direction**: these four elements each work hand in hand to give an accent solid foundations.

Below we have given brief descriptions of the foundations of six example accents from the CD.

As you listen to the six examples, use your new skills of seeing, feeling and hearing the zone, tone, setting and direction.

It is hard to describe a tonal quality on paper. It is the quality that *you hear* that counts. We have used words that describe the tones we hear and what those tones reminded us of. You may well think of other things…

	ZONE	TONE	SETTING AND HESITATION		DIRECTION
Standard English (RP) [TRACK 96]	2	Soft and Velvety.	Loose jaw. Slight lift in top lip. Soft palate high and bouncy. Tongue tip active, often flicking up to gum-ridge.	**'UHM'**	Forward out of the mouth like a wave, avoiding all obstacles on the way!
Cockney [TRACK 95]	3	Brass Band.	Jaw held. Lips flat and thin. Soft palate low.	**'AM'**	Punched up onto the hard palate and forward onto the teeth.
Liverpool [TRACK 92]	4	Foghorn.	Jaw held close. Cheeks and lips wide. Soft palate low. Tongue held high.	**'E..M'**	Spilling sideways.
Glasgow [TRACK 89]	5	The sound of effortful lifting!	Cheeks loose. Lips slightly lifted and pouting. Tongue rolled forward and squeezed into EE position. Soft palate low.	**'EYM'**	Falling backwards.
Manchester [TRACK 91]	6	Trumpet with mute.	Back of tongue high, soft palate low.	**'OEM'**	Held at the back and circling.
Newcastle [TRACK 90]	5 – 3	Swedish Chef!	Cheeks and lips move suddenly between shapes. Back on tongue tense and raised. Jaw held and jumpy.	**'EM'**	Lurching back and forth.

HOW TO DO ACCENTS

The Foundations Checklist

Now when you are working on any accent be sure to identify:

- What **Zone** does it focus into?
- What is the **Tone** I need?
- What does the **Setting** feel like?
- In what **Direction** does the sound travel out of the mouth?

You and the New

Now's the time to use the **You and the New** chart at the back of the book. Using a recording of yourself, or someone with your accent, identify the elements of your own foundation and put them in the 'Foundations' section of the chart. This way you will be able to see how any new accent compares to your own.

TOP TIP ────────────────────────────────────

*Remember, at this stage you are only listening for the **Zone**, **Tone**, **Setting** and **Direction**. You may well notice other things, but don't be distracted by all the other elements that make up an accent. These are just the foundations!*

3

THE TWO PLANETS

(Rhotic v Non-Rhotic)

IN THIS CHAPTER...

You will discover about **rhoticity** (and no, that isn't a way of cooking a chicken). When it comes to accents the world divides into two planets:

- **Rhotic** – People who *always* say an R *whenever* it is written –
  ORDER MOTHER CART HERE
- **Non-rhotic** – People who *only* say an R if there is a vowel sound *spoken* after it –
  HARRY HERO BRING SACRED RIGHT

More significantly you'll discover which planet *you* are on, and how to pass as a local on the other!

There was a time when English was all on one planet: Planet Rhotic. That's why the R's are there in the written word. But over time the world divided in two...

On Planet Rhotic life is simple: every R that they see, they say! ('Of course we do!' the Rhotics cry.)

On Planet Non-Rhotic, however, life is a bit more complicated. Here speakers only pronounce an R if it is directly followed by a spoken vowel sound. So they pronounce the R in *run, horrid, flowery,* but not in *heart, far* or *flower*. What was historically a vowel plus R will often be said as a **long vowel**, making HEART become HAAHT, and CAR become CAH.

So who's on which planet? Well, on Planet Rhotic you have most speakers of **American English**, **Barbados**, **Canada**, **India**, **Ireland** and **Scotland**, the English **West Country**, and parts of **Lancashire**.

On Planet Non-Rhotic you will find **Africa**, **Australia**, most of the **Caribbean**, most of **England**, most of **New Zealand** and **Wales**, many North East coast American accents, such as **New York City** and **Boston** as well as some older accents of the deep south of America, as well as many African American accents. **Singapore** and **Malaysia** are also two examples of countries in Asia with a non-rhotic accent, while in Canada non-rhotic accents have been reported in south-western **New Brunswick**, various isolated parts of **Newfoundland**, and **Lunenburg County, Nova Scotia**.

This can lead to confusion as we move from planet to planet, as Edda found when giving her surname to register at a Canadian hotel. She pronounced 'SHARPE' the English way, 'SHAHP'. Looking down she saw the receptionist write the word, 'SHOP'!

Which planet are you on?

Look at the phrase: Law and Order.

- How many R's do you see?
- How many R's do you *say?*

Some of you will be saying two R's, both in the word Order. But others of you may only be saying one R, and you'll be saying it where there isn't even one written, like this: law r-and. What's more, you probably don't even realise you're doing it! That's what we mean by two planets.

Still not sure which planet you're on? Say the *name* of this letter the way you normally would when reciting the alphabet: **R**.

Do you *feel* your tongue move to shape an R? Then your accent is on Planet Rhotic!

Or does it stay open, making more of an 'AH'? Then your accent is on Planet Non-Rhotic!

If your own accent follows a rhotic pattern:

- It is the non-rhotic accents that will be more challenging, so if you want to cut to the chase go to page 53 for 'Spotlight on Planet Non-Rhotic' and learn the funny ways of those non-rhotic people!

If your own accent follows a non-rhotic pattern:

- For you, rhotic accents will be very challenging, so you need to look carefully at 'Spotlight on Planet Rhotic' below.

But there's nothing to stop you reading about your own pattern – remember, knowing your own funny quirks can help you understand why a new accent may be going awry!

Spotlight on Planet Rhotic

The first rule on Planet Rhotic is:

- If you see an R you say it…and if you don't, *don't!*

That sounds straightforward, but here are two big mistakes that non-rhotic speakers make when doing rhotic accents that *always* give them away:

- Leaving out R's that should be there.

- Adding ones that shouldn't be there.

And believe us, non-rhotics will often do this without even realising.

So here's how to avoid those two killer mistakes.

How to put in R's that *should* be there

The way that words are written reflects the rhotic view of the world (and it certainly confirms that once upon a time *all* English speakers were rhotic). Basically, if there is an R in the spelling of a word, a rhotic speaker will *always* say it.

See It

Look at this sentence. We have highlighted all the R's in it. To be rhotic you will need to say all these R's!

MaRgaRet caught heR daughteR pouRing wateR oveR the floweRs.

Hear It [TRACK 5]
- Listen to the CD of our three rhotic speakers saying this sentence and hear how all the R's are spoken.
  - *Scottish*
  - *Standard American*
  - *Northern Irish*

Notice that although the *way* they say the R is different (in this case Tap, Molar, Retroflex – more about these terms in 'Spotlight on R', page 61), *when* they say it is the same. That's Planet Rhotic.

Feel It
- Choose an R that feels familiar and comfortable to do. Remember, for the purpose of this exercise it doesn't matter which kind of R you use, so long as you are aware of *when* you are saying it! If you want to be more specific you will of course need to learn the right *kind* of R for the accent you are doing… (More about that in 'Spotlight on R', page 61).

HOW TO DO ACCENTS

- Speak the sentence yourself, saying all the R's in the same places as the rhotic speakers. That simply means wherever one is written.

TOP TIP

- *Words with an R will now take a little longer to say because there is an extra movement for your tongue to make. So slow down!*

SATURDAY

- *Your tongue isn't familiar with the new movement, especially when it has to happen quickly. Practise the move to make it fluent and easy.*

CORNER

How *not* to add R's that *shouldn't* be there!

One of the biggest mistakes non-rhotic people make when doing a rhotic accent (such as Standard American) is to *add* R's where they *shouldn't*. If you're an American you'll know how annoying that is, and many of us Brits don't even know we've done it!

When doing an American accent you may be quite happy to buy a 'pizzar in American', but of course, you would be wrong. So why do we do it? Well, in non-rhotic accents, the dropped R means that many words rhyme that wouldn't if we kept the R. Look at these pairs of words and you'll see what we mean:

Court Caught   Pour Paw   Sore Saw   Sort Sought

In a non-rhotic accent the two words in these pairs sound the same. Here lies the root of the problem. Once a non-rhotic successfully learns to put the R in the first word, they will automatically want to put one in the second, thus keeping the same sound… Mistake! This is your non-rhotic sound pattern at work, and *not* the pattern of your new accent. In a rhotic accent these words sound completely different. A non-rhotic may think it sounds fine, but to a rhotic ear it will sound at best confusing and at worst comical.

Now look at these two lists: same problem, different sound!

Actor   Brother   Wilbur   Author
Linda   Pizza   America   Plaza

Again, in non-rhotic accents these words all end with the same small UH sound (called the **schwa** – see page 124), and once you have learned to put an R on the end of the first set you may find yourself putting R's on the second set too! But in rhotic accents they are *completely different*! This may seem obvious, but try it and you will see how hard it can sometimes be.

Feel It

- Say **Court**, pronouncing the R.
- Say **Caught**, without an R.
- Say the two words one after the other, ensuring that one has an R and one doesn't.

Do this a few times to get used to this new pattern. Break the rhyme!

Now put them in this sentence: **I caught the bus to go to court**.

Now try these:

- Say **Wilbur**, pronouncing the final R
- Say **Linda**, without adding a final R!
- Say them a few times feeling the different ending.

And now put it all together in this sentence: **Linda caught Wilbur in court**.

And just when you thought you'd cracked it…

You will also need to learn the rhotic way of gliding from one vowel to another across two words *without* inserting an R!

Say these phrases and notice if you have even a slight urge to put an R between the words where we've marked them. Maybe you don't notice yourself do it. Get another non-rhotic person to say them and listen to what they do.

Linda and I   Law and Justice
Linda **R**and I   Law **R**and Justice

A rhotic speaker would simply *never* do this! Not only do they not do this, they find it extremely noticeable and baffling when they hear other people do it.

Here's what to do:

Feel It

- Glide from one word to the other, maintaining the open shape at the end of one word and the beginning of the other, keeping the tip of the tongue relaxed behind the bottom teeth.

HOW TO DO ACCENTS

- It can really help to think of the second word as part of the first:

  Lindaand I   Lawnd Justice

This is what the rhotics do!

To do any rhotic accent it is *vital* to practise these glides, as *all* rhotic accents use them.

Practise your new R patterns on this sentence. Remember to put in R's that should be there and not to put in R's that shouldn't!

Wilbur told his daughter (not DOOR-ter!) Linda (not lindER!) to talk about law and (not LORand!) justice, but it bored her. He had an awesome (not OARsome!) idea (not ideaR!)

This is the pattern that you need to be rhotic, look out for R's like a hork – oops, we mean *hawk*. Don't let that non-rhotic rhyme pattern lead you into mistakes. After all, it's important to distinguish 'the dog's paw' from 'the dog's pore'…

Spotlight on Planet Non-Rhotic

Okay, rhotic folk! Gone are the simple days when an R was simply said wherever it appeared in a word.

> On Planet Non-Rhotic you can think of the R in two ways:
> - *Only ever* say an R if it is *followed* by a vowel sound.
> - *Never* say an R if it is *followed* by a consonant.

See It

- Look at this word: **Cargo**
  Although there's an R written, it's followed by a consonant, so *don't say* it!
- And this word: **Order**
  There are two R's written here; the first R is followed by a consonant (D) and the second R ends the word, so *don't say* them!
- Now look at this word: **Hero**
  This R is followed by a vowel sound, so *do say* it!

- And what about this word? **Hairy**

  Although the Y looks like a consonant it is spoken here as a vowel sound, so..this R is followed by a vowel so *do say* it!
- And what about these teasers? **Here Care**

  It may look like the R is followed by a vowel, but it isn't a *spoken vowel* so bang goes the R: *don't say* it!

How to lose those R's

Hear It [TRACK 6]

Listen to these non-rhotic speakers saying the following words without pronouncing the R's.

- *Norfolk, Wales, Newcastle:*

  Park   Stern   Here   Poor   Hair   Court

Feel It

- Say the words yourself, losing the R's *completely*.
- Instead of the R, just lengthen the vowel.
- Keep the tip of your tongue behind your bottom teeth.

See It

Look in the mirror. Check that you are not contracting *any muscles* for that non-existent R.

Be careful: your tongue may *think* it's not doing an R, and maybe it doesn't sound like an R to you, but is your tongue still moving? Even a little bit? Even the *slightest* movement of the tongue, however small, will still be heard as an R by a non-rhotic speaker. It really does need to be dropped *completely*!

> **TOP TIP**
> *We have found that it can really help rhotic people to re-write the words without an R in the spelling, and to see the words this way:*
> **Mahgret pawed the watuh   Richud loved flowuh powuh**

HOW TO DO ACCENTS

Feel It

Now practise on this little paragraph. Remember the rule: if it's followed by a vowel *sound* you say it; if it's not you don't!

Margaret, Rhys and Richard poured water all over the flowers, they loved pouring water.

So that's how to lose those R's... Now for when to put them back in!

Doing the R bounce

Because a non-rhotic R is only said when followed by a vowel it is no longer just a letter in a word, it now has a special job to do: it's a springboard off which the vowel can jump, giving a bounce to the start of syllables! This results in these three great features of non-rhotic accents:

- The **mid-word bounce** (see below): Gerry = Ge-rry
- The **linking bounce** (page 56): Car alarm = Ca-ralarm
- The **intrusive bounce** (page 57): Linda and I = Linda – rand I

The mid-word bounce

Look at these words with R's in the middle:

Very   Sorry   Harry   Worry   Spirit   Courage

For many people on Planet Rhotic the R is part of the first syllable and the two syllables glide into one another:

Ver–y   Sorr–y   Harr–y   Worr–y   Spir–it   Cour–age

But on Planet Non-Rhotic the R is used to bounce into the second syllable. The syllables are clearly separated. The vowel before the R must be kept absolutely clean of any influence from the R that follows it!

Ve – ry   So – rry   Ha – rry   Wo – rry   Spi – rit   Cou – rage

Hear It [TRACK 7]
- *American:* rhotic
- *Standard English (RP):* non-rhotic

Feel It

Speak the example words yourself slowly and carefully, feeling the separation of the syllables, keeping the R clear of the preceding vowel and using the R to bounce into the following syllable.

Ve – ry   So – rry   Ha – rry   Wo – rry   Spi – rit   Cou – rage

The linking bounce

As we have seen, when an R *ends* a word a non-rhotic speaker won't say it because it's not followed by a spoken vowel:

Car   More   Here

However, if the next word *starts with a vowel*…then the R has its job back! The non-rhotic speaker 'links' the two words with the R. It is important to note that this R does not *end* the first word, but bounces into the second:

Car **R**alarm   More **R**over   Here **R**I am

 Hear (r)It [TRACK 8]

Listen to these speakers from *Norfolk*, *Liverpool* and *Newcastle* dropping the R when the word is on its own, but using it to link to the next word!
- Car   Car **R**alarm
- More   More **R**over
- Here   Here **R**I am

 Feel It

- First say the word on its own without the R.
- Now put the words together using the R to start the following word *without breaking the flow.*

And try this phrase with the linking bounces marked:

John tipped water ʳinto the plants, more ʳover Wilbur ʳand Linda didn't!

TOP TIP ————————————————————————————————

*Watch out! This **won't** happen if the speaker breaks the flow or breathes between the words!*

Dropping the R often makes rhotic speakers feel so good in their new non-rhotic accent that they do it too much, missing the authenticity that the linking bounce can give.

———

HOW TO DO ACCENTS

And here's the final and somewhat cheeky little bounce…

The intrusive bounce

On Planet Non-Rhotic, just because there's no R written, it doesn't mean you can't do one.

Some non-rhotics just *hate* having two vowel sounds next to each other. They feel they just *have* to insert a consonant to help with the flow!

For some non-rhotic speakers, it can feel entirely natural to insert an R to make a cheeky little bounce from one vowel to another!

Edda and Jan = 'Edda **R**and Jan'.

This is often referred to as an Intrusive R, because the *sound* of an R intrudes where there is no *written* R. (Cheeky!)

It is most often used to bounce between two words:

India **R**and China   Draw **R**out   Linda **R**is

And it can even happen *within* a word…

Paw**R**ing   Draw**R**ing

…which can make the words **Pouring** and **Pawing** sound exactly the same!

Hear It [TRACK 9]

● *Norfolk, West Midlands, Yorkshire:*

Linda **R**is draw**R**ing India **R**and China

However odd it sounds to you, it is so natural to many non-rhotic speakers that they don't even know they are doing it!

Feel It

● Have a go yourself inserting a gentle R to bounce from one vowel to the other.

Here are some more phrases to play with:

● I saw a boy becomes I saw **R**a boy

● I had an idea about that becomes I had an idea **R**about that

● Linda and I sat in the drawing room becomes
Linda **R**and I sat in the draw**R**ing room

Yes, people really do this! It is a very common feature of non-rhotic accents such as London, Liverpool and New York.

It is not a feature of *all* non-rhotic accents, however. Some accents of the deep south of America don't do it and the 'posher' speakers of Standard English (RP) frown on it!

When it comes to rhoticity, getting it right or wrong can really make or break your accent. There are some accents that are 'hybrids'. This happens when one accent becomes influenced by another from the other planet. The American South is losing many of its non-rhotic accents, for example, while Dublin and much of the South West of England are losing their rhoticity. Sometimes the dominant patterns of the country begin to take over the smaller accent pockets; sometimes social aspiration or association means that an accent will change. When you hear a hybrid, be extra careful to notice which R's are kept and which are lost. This is why it is so important to know the background of any accent you wish to learn.

Rhoticity Checklist

Is the accent rhotic (always an R) or non-rhotic (only an R before a vowel sound)?

- **Rhotic**?

  See 'Spotlight on R' (page 61) to check what kind of R they use.

- **Non-rhotic**?

  - Do they use a **Linking Bounce**: Car **R**alarm

  - Do they use an **Intrusive Bounce**: Law **R**and order

  See 'Spotlight on R' (page 61) to check what kind of R they use.

You and the New

Is your own accent rhotic or non-rhotic? Do you use a linking bounce or an intrusive bounce? Go to the 'You and the New' chart at the end of the book and make a note of your patterns so that you can compare any new accent to your own. If your new accent is on the opposite planet from yours, you will need to be extra vigilant.

HOW TO DO ACCENTS

4

THE BITE

(Consonants)

IN THIS CHAPTER...

You will discover the impact that consonants can have on an accent and the significant ways in which consonants differ from region to region.

We have identified the five **Major Players**: a set of consonants with the power to make or break your accent. Get these wrong and you risk your whole accent going down the pan! You cannot ignore the fact that Belfast uses a strong R, for example; the R must be said and said strongly. Ignore this fact and bang goes your Belfast.

The five Major Players are:

- **R** – tapping, bending, curling or bunching?
- **L** – light, dark, or not at all?
- **H** – to drop or not to drop?
- **NG** – are you running, runnin' runn'n or runningk for the bus?
- **TH** – are you with it, wivvit, widdit or wizzit?

Each of these Major Players is governed by patterns, 'rules' that determine both *how* to say them and also *when* to say them. The L alone can take you from one region to another if you don't get it right, as this little anecdote demonstrates...

Edda was asked to solve a problem for an actor whose own accent was strongly Lancashire. He was playing a character from the South Wales Valleys. Now, Lancashire is renowned for its heavy, dark L and the Welsh Valleys for its delicate light L . He found the vowels of the valleys particularly seductive and had great fun using them, but he had completely overlooked the consonants. Consequently he was speaking his new accent with South Welsh vowels and Lancashire consonants. The curious result had been that a Welsh woman in the audience complemented him on his North Wales accent! It was a seemingly small error, but it was enough to move him a hundred miles north.

We have also identified the **Major Issues** that can affect the sound and quality of all consonants. You will not only discover the powerful impact they can have on the overall quality of an accent, but you will also begin to develop the muscular flexibility to make those all-important changes.

Finally we take a look at a cheeky set of consonants we call the **Springing Consonants**. These are 'consonants in vowels' clothing' and can pop up where you least expect them!

The Major Players

So here they are, introducing those five make-or-break sounds…

R – tapping, bending, curling or bunching?

L – light, dark, or not at all?

H – to drop or not to drop?

NG – are you running, runnin' runn'n or runningk for the bus?

TH – are you with it, wivvit, widdit or wizzit?

Get these wrong and you risk your whole accent going down the pan!

It's time to shine the…

Spotlight on R

What makes this a Major Player is…

There are just so many different ways to make an R. To do an authentic accent you need to know *which type* of R an accent uses, when it uses it and how to do it.

Did you know different types of R's have names? How about doing a 'retroflex R', a 'tap' or 'trill'? What about a 'rabbity R', or maybe you'd prefer to get your teeth round a 'molar R'?

How the R is made, the speed at which it moves, the zone it sits in and whether or not it touches the roof of the mouth: these will all have a dramatic effect, not just on the pronunciation of the word, but on the overall quality of the accent.

As we go through each of these R's, don't worry about the vowel shapes you are using, or making a specific accent, but if an accent seems to appear in your mouth as a result of making the R, then go with it!

Taps and trills

A tapped R is made when the tongue makes rapid contact with the roof of the mouth. If your tongue taps more than once in succession then you have made a trill! Taps are found in many English accents like Liverpool and the North of England, as well as Welsh and Scottish accents: these all use tapped R's to a greater or lesser extent. Trills, on the other hand, tend to be more prevalent in accents rooted in languages other than English. Accents of English which use a trill will often use a simple tap when speaking rapidly or casually, and save a trill for more careful or emphatic speech. This is true of some African, Welsh and Scottish accents for example.

How to do a gum-ridge tap

In a gum-ridge tap the tongue-tip lifts up and 'taps' the gum-ridge. It's a little like doing a quick, light D.

Hear It [TRACK 10]

This is the sound of a gum-ridge tap:

- *Liverpool:* Margaret and Gerry were very rowdy after drinking the terrible water.

See It

Feel It

If your tongue doesn't know what to do to make a gum-ridge tap, take it through the following steps:

- Lift the tip of your tongue up to your gum-ridge and tap it there lightly. This is the target in the mouth that the tongue needs to aim for.

HOW TO DO ACCENTS

- Whisper a long 'AAHH', breath only, and while breathing out make the gentlest tap you can, without breaking the flow of air. It will sound a little like: *'AHHDAHH'*.
- Now, aim the tip of your tongue to your gum-ridge in these words, as if about to do a very light, gentle D, and let the tip make a quick flick against the ridge. Whisper the words first to focus on the feeling and the movement, and then use full voice. Use the tip of the tongue to flick into the next syllable.

Gerry   Very   Drinking   Terrible

How to do a retroflex tap

If you curl the tip of the tongue a little further back and tap behind the gum-ridge you have a 'retroflex tap'! This is the R heard in most accents derived from the Indian Sub-Continent.

Hear It [TRACK 11]

- *Punjabi:* Margaret and Gerry were very rowdy after drinking the terrible water.

Tapped R's can be found in both rhotic and non-rhotic accents, so make sure you try both patterns.

When an accent chooses to use a tapped R will often depend on the other sounds that surround it.

> **TOP TIP**
>
> *Always check the specifics of **when** to tap. Some non-rhotic accents only tap between vowels, for example, and most accents don't tap R's that **start** words.*

How to do a uvular tap, trill or fricative

Although this is an unusual sound for English speakers, some older speakers from the North East of England and North Wales do use this sound in their accents. It is also quite common in other languages, such as French, German and Dutch.

For a uvular R the *back* of the tongue arches up and bounces off the soft palate.

Hear It [TRACK 12]

This is the sound of a uvular R:

- _Old Newcastle:_ Margaret and Gerry were very rowdy after drinking the terrible water.

 See It

 Feel It

- Hold your tongue _almost_ in a G position.
- Keep your _throat relaxed_.
- Say 'AH'.
- Gently bounce the softest G you can make off the soft palate.

Have a go using a uvular R on this practice sentence:

Margaret and Gerry were very rowdy after drinking the terrible water.

Your tongue may learn this quickly, but some tongues find it tricky. Work on the movement and sound in isolation.

Don't let it fall back into the throat, but keep it in the springy part of the tongue and soft palate. Be patient!

When this sound is repeated in quick succession you have a uvular trill. This is the sound of a purr, or Eartha Kitt!

Bends, curls and bunches

The important thing with bends, curls and bunches is which _part_ of your tongue does the bending, curling or bunching and which _zone_ you resonate the sound in. Listen to accents of South West England, North America and Ireland and you'll hear all sorts of bending, curling and bunching R's.

Far back in the mouth you can find bunched molar R's, retroflex R's curl up towards the roof of the mouth, while a slight bend by the gum-ridge makes a free R. If it's not the tongue that bends at all, but the bottom lip instead, you have a little sound called an R substitute.

Let's begin at the back of the mouth with the bunched-up molar R.

How to do bunched molar R's

The molar R is a strong feature of many North American accents, and it is often where English actors come unstuck.

The tongue body is retracted, the *sides* of the tongue press up and out against the top molars and the tip bunches back, disappearing into the body of the tongue.

Hear It [TRACK 13]

This is the sound of a molar R:

- *American:* Margaret and Gerry were very rowdy after drinking the terrible water.

See It

Feel It

- Pull your tongue back and lift it up to scrape the sides along your top molars. Feel how the tongue bunches up.

See It

- Look in the mirror as you do this and see how the tongue is pressed up in the mouth, while the tip disappears into the body of the tongue, which is drawn back in the mouth.

Hear It

- Holding the tongue in that position, make the sound 'HRRR'.

That's a molar R. It is a very muscular action for the tongue to do, and if your tongue is not used to it, it may take a while to develop the agility to make this movement quickly. Try it on this sentence:

Margaret and Gerry were very rowdy after drinking the terrible water.

The molar R in different zones

Did you know it is possible to focus your molar R into the different **zones** in your mouth? North Americans are especially sensitive to to the type of R they are hearing. Each region of America has its own special R resonance. Being able to move your molar R into different zones will enable you to move your accent from region to region across North America, giving you a fantastic key to accessing and anchoring the difference between Newfoundland and Ontario, Texas and California.

Feel It and Hear It

- Push the tongue up against the molars and slide it back and forth.
- Add voice to this slide and focus your sound into different zones.
- Hear how the resonance changes as you do this.
- Isolate different spots to stop off at in zones 2, 3 and 4 and listen to each of them in turn.

How to do curled retroflex R's

The roof of the mouth is home to the retroflex R. It can be heard in Northern Ireland and accents of the West of England and Central Lancashire. It may be fully retroflex, or it may be bunching back with just a little curl of the tip. To do a full retroflex R, the tongue tip curls right up and back in the mouth; the jaw is held a little open and the lips tend to round. (*Retro* = 'back'; *flex* = 'curl'.)

Retroflex R's tend to resonate quite strongly. The focus of that resonance can be anywhere from the middle to the back of the mouth, in zones 3, 4, 5, or 6, depending on the degree of curling and retraction of the tongue. They can be made with or without 'nasal spill' (see page 122)!

Hear It [TRACK 14]

This is the sound of a retroflex R:

- *Northern Irish:* Margaret and Gerry were very rowdy after drinking the terrible water.

See It

Feel It

- Curl the tongue tip back and growl strongly.
- Focus the resonance in different places in different zones in the mouth – 3, 4, 5 and 6 – as you curl back the tongue.
- Now use a retroflex R on the sentence:

  Margaret and Gerry were very rowdy after drinking the terrible water

This is also a very muscular action for the tongue to perform, and if it's not used to it, it may take a while to develop the agility to make this movement quickly.

How to do bending Free R's

Moving to the front of the mouth we find the free R. This is the R used in many *Southern* (but not Northern) Irish accents and most English accents.

Although the whole *body* of the tongue does not retract, bunch or curl, the *tip* is doing a lot of work. The tip curls or bends up towards the gum-ridge, without actually touching it. The cheeks may pull in to 'support' the tongue. The sound resonates in the mouth, neither on the back of the tongue nor spilling down the nose. If your own R is a substitute (see below) this will feel like work, but if your own R is a strong molar or retroflex this may not feel like an R at all!

 Hear It [TRACK 15]

> This is the sound of a free R.
> * *Southern Irish:* Margaret and Gerry were very rowdy after drinking the terrible water.

 See It

 Feel It

> * Curl the tip of your tongue up towards your gum-ridge, without actually touching it.
> * Keep it curling up and add your voice to this shape.
> * Focus the sound onto the gum-ridge.
> * The cheeks may pull in to support the shape.

Now use this free R in the sentence:

> Margaret and Gerry were very rowdy after drinking the terrible water.

Getting this free R will be *especially* important for Northern Irish and North Americans if they want to travel to England and Southern Ireland.

HOW TO DO ACCENTS

R Substitute

We have been moving the R from the back of the mouth to the front, starting with the molar, through the retroflex R and forward to the free R. Any further forward and the R will fall out of the mouth and land on the teeth and lips – and that is just what happens with the R substitute! Because it is effectively outside the mouth, it doesn't resonate in *any* of the zones.

You may be familiar with the terms 'weak R', or a 'rabbity R'. There's a great example of one in the film *The Life of Brian*, when Michael Palin's Pontius Pilate calls to the crowd: 'Welease Woger!'. That is what we mean by an R substitute! In an R substitute the tongue doesn't move at all: instead, it hands the job of making the R over to the lips and teeth to form a kind of V or W. Some *individuals* have such a 'weak' R that their R substitute is indistinguishable from a W! Good examples of accents that use substitutes are New York City and the East End of London.

Hear It [TRACK 16]

This is the sound of an R substitute:

- *London:* Margaret and Gerry were very rowdy after drinking the terrible water.

See It

Feel It

- Relax the tongue *completely*!
- Lift the inside of your bottom lip towards your top front teeth.
- Focus the sound onto the bottom lip.

Use this R substitute in the sentence:

> Margaret and Gerry were very rowdy after drinking the terrible water.

Try the sentence as a Cockney, or imagine you are from New York City and you'll hear what a difference this sound can make.

So that's the R. Now when you are listening to a new accent, listen for this Major Player and ask yourself:

Q: How is the R made?

Q: Where does it tap, bend, curl or bunch to?

Q: Which **zone** does it resonate in?

Q: How long does it last?

Q: Is it always the same R or does it depend on the sounds around it?

Each accent will have its own special combination. It may be a rhotic accent with a trill, or a non-rhotic accent with a tap, it may tap between vowels, but bend everywhere else. Whichever R combination you use in your own accent, the chances are that other accents use a *different* combination. Now you can see just what a Major Player R really is!

The sentence below will quickly illustrate what kind of R is used when by you and/or your speaker.

> R: Margaret, Linda and Gerry asked Peter if Roland started with 'R'.

You and the New

Whichever R you use in your own accent, the chances are that other accents use a different one. Identify the way you make your own R's and the way your new accent makes theirs and make a note in the **You and the New** chart at the back of the book.

HOW TO DO ACCENTS

Spotlight on L

If ever there was a **Major Player** this is it! This seemingly innocent little sound is capable of transporting your accent from one place to another all on its own!

What makes this a Major Player is...

- **There are in fact three types of L: Light, Dark and W Substitute.**
- **There are *four* L patterns: accents that use...**
  1. **Only light L**
  2. **Only dark L**
  3. **Light and dark L combination**
  4. **Light L or dark L, plus W substitute combination**

Hear It [TRACK 17]

Listen to the following accent examples, each using a different L pattern. Listen especially to the quality of the L's in each example:

> Larry the lazy lamb slept peacefully in the field until hailstones fell.

- Only light L: *Welsh*
  Light L uses only the front of the tongue, and it feels and sounds light and delicate.
- Only dark L: *Manchester*
  Dark L, on the other hand, uses the front *and back* of the tongue and feels and sounds heavy and muscular.
- Light and dark L combination: *Standard Southern English*
  These accents use a combination of the above two L's:
- Light L and W substitute: *London*
  Dark L and W substitute: *American Deep South*
  These accents use a combination of L's, but W substitute replaces the dark L before a consonant or at the end of a word. For W substitute the front of the tongue is *not used at all*, the back of the tongue raises and the lips round, making a W-like sound.

To do any accent you will need to know *how* to do each of the different L's and *when* to use them! Remember, they can make or break your accent.

So here's how to do them…

Light L

Hear It [TRACK 18]

Listen to us say the sentence using only light L's and have a go yourself.

Larry the lazy lamb slept peacefully in the field until hailstones fell.

See It

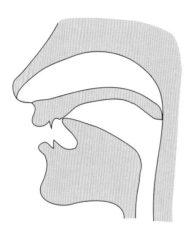

The essential quality of a light L is that *only the front of the tongue* is used to make it.

The 'lightness' is variable from 'quite light' to 'extremely light'. This will depend on how much of the front of the tongue makes contact: the less tongue used, the lighter the sound!

Look in the mirror…

- Stick your tongue out and point it up to the middle of your top lip.
- See the way the tongue narrows, points and curls up.
- Keeping the shape, draw the tongue into the mouth and place the pointy tip onto the gum-ridge.

Feel It

- Hold this shape.
- Feel the open space at the back of your mouth and the tensing of the front of the tongue.
- Breathe out through this shape, thinking the vowel EE.
- Add your voice to this shape and you have a light L!
- Practise getting your tongue to and from this position:
  Leeleeleelee looloolooolooloo laalaalaalaa (etc).

HOW TO DO ACCENTS

Hear It

- Listen to the quality of the sound you are making.
- Listen to us again (TRACK 18)…does your L sound the same?

So that's a light L. Many accents use *only* a light L: those of the Indian Sub-continent, most of Wales, all of Ireland and the far North East of England are all light L only accents. If your own accent doesn't use a light L your tongue will be learning a whole new shape. Keep practising the muscularity and sound until your tongue is confident forming it.

TOP TIP

Ever wondered why when you try to do Newcastle you sometimes sound Welsh, or when you try Welsh you sound Indian? They all use light L!

Dark L

Hear It [TRACK 19]

Listen to us doing the sentence using dark L's and have a go yourself.

Larry the lazy lamb slept peacefully in the field until hailstones fell.

See It

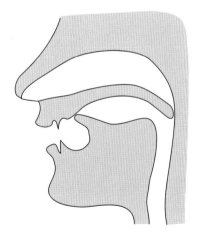

The essential quality of a dark L is that as well as the tongue tip touching the gum-ridge, the *back of the tongue is raised towards the soft palate.*

The 'darkness' is variable, from 'quite dark' to 'extremely dark'. This will depend on just how much of the back of the tongue rises. It is this added muscularity that can make the dark L tricky, especially if you are not used to it.

Feel It

- Place your tongue tip on your gum-ridge and 'glue' it there.
- Hold the position and go to say an 'OO' sound…the back of the tongue raises towards a G position. This is the essential feature of a dark L.

- Hold all the internal muscles in place, but lose the lip-rounding!
- Practise getting to and from this position.

  lloolloolloolloolloo llaallaallaallaa lleelleelleellee (etc).

Hear It

- Listen to the quality of the sound you are making.
- Listen to us again (TRACK 18)…does your dark L sound the same?

So that's a dark L. Many accents use *only* a dark L: Scottish, the North of England, North America and Australia are all dark L only accents. If your own accent doesn't use a dark L, either because you only use light L or because your dark L is in fact a W substitute, you will be teaching your tongue a new shape. Keep practising the muscularity and sound until your tongue is confident.

If your new accent is a single L accent, life is pretty simple: you will need to use just one L all the time, be it dark or light. But there are many accents that prefer to mix and match their L's (all of the South of England, for example). For these accents you need to know not only how to do each L but also which one to use when.

Light plus Dark L

For these accents you will need to be able to do *both* the light and the dark L!

The light L is only used if it is followed by a vowel sound.

- At the beginning of a word: Look   Light
- Separating syllables: Toilet   Silly
- On the end of a word if the next word starts with a vowel:
  Hill‿and Dale   Fall‿Over

The dark L is used everywhere else!

- On the end of a word where no vowel follows it: Hill
- Before a consonant sound: Field

HOW TO DO ACCENTS

Hear It [TRACK 20]

Listen to us using both L's in the following sentence and then have a go yourself. Listen for the shift from light to dark L. We have helped you by indicating all the light L's in *italics* and all the dark L's in **bold**:

*L*arry the *l*azy *l*amb s*l*ept peacefu*ll*y in the fie**l**d unti**l** hai**l**stones fe**ll**.

Feel It

- Say these words using a light L:

  Larry   Lazy   Slept   Peacefully

- Say these words using a dark L:

  Field   Until   Hailstones   Fell

- Say these words starting with a light L and finishing each word with a dark L:

  Lull   Little

So that's the light L + dark L combination. This combination is an essential element in the accent of Standard English (RP) and many other accents in the South of England. If your own accent doesn't have this pattern there are two L's to get your mouth around and you will need to be on your toes about which one to use when!

Light L or Dark L plus W Substitute Combination

These accents follow the same pattern as light L + dark L combinations.

> **The light L or dark L is only used if it is followed by a vowel sound.**
>
> - At the beginning of a word: Look   Light
> - Separating syllables: Toilet   Silly
> - On the end of a word if the next word starts with a vowel:
>
>   Hill‿and Dale   Fall‿Over
>
> **The W substitute is used everywhere else!**
>
> - On the end of a word where no vowel follows it: Hill
> - Before a consonant sound: Field

Of course this pattern involves a whole new speech sound: the W substitute. So here's how to do it…

W Substitute

 Hear It [TRACK 21]

> Listen to us saying the same sentence, only this time using the W substitute in place of the dark L's.
>
> Larry the *lazy l*amb s*l*ept peacefu*ll*y in the fie*l*d unti*l* hai*l*stones fe*ll*

 See It

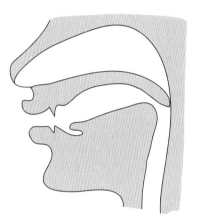

The essential quality of a W substitute is that the *tip of the tongue doesn't lift up to the gum-ridge at all*. The back of the tongue lifts as with dark L, and the lips round.

 Feel It

- Say the word **Well** and instead of saying the L replace it with the W you had at the beginning of the word, making an OO like sound: WE-OO.
- Make sure you *don't* use your tongue tip at all.
- Mouth the word silently, again replacing the L with a W.

 See It

- Do the above looking in the mirror and watch the movement of the lips as they round.

 Hear It

- Listen to the OO quality in the sound.

HOW TO DO ACCENTS

- Listen to the sound we used in the sentence (TRACK 21) and make sure yours sounds the same!

Practise the movement and sound on these words:

Hill   Field   Ball   Bottle

Now practise the pattern on this paragraph, using light L for the letters in *italics* and W substitute for the words in **bold**:

*L*arry the *l*azy *l*amb s*l*ept peacefu*ll*y in the field unti**l** hailstones fe**ll** heavi*l*y from the c*l*ouds. '*Sl*eeping is impossible!' he wailed. *L*assie the sheep-dog called *l*oud*l*y: '*L*ift your *l*azy *l*egs Larry and come out of the cold field into this *l*ove*l*y warm she**l**ter'.

So that's the light L or dark L + W substitute.

The sentence below will quickly illustrate which L pattern you and/or your speaker uses.

   L: Larry the silly lamb slept peacefully in the field until hailstones fell.

You and the New

That's all the L possibilities. (Well, we did say it was a Major Player...) So do you know which L pattern you use? What about your new accent? Chances are they are very different. Make a note in the **You and the New** chart at the back of the book.

Spotlight on H

What makes this a Major Player is...
When there is an H at the start of a word some accents will say it ('H-doing') and others will not ('H-dropping').

Compared to the other Major Players H-doing or dropping is relatively easy, but it is no less important and still *key* to creating an authentic detailed accent.

Hear It [TRACK 22]

Listen to these two speakers saying this sentence. The first is from *Newcastle* and is an H-doer; the second is speaking in a traditional *Cockney* accent and is an H-dropper.

Harry Hobson had a holiday in Hawaii

Say the sentence yourself in your own accent. Are you an H-doer or dropper?

H-doers	H-droppers
If you are *not* a natural H-dropper it is *really* worth getting on top of this feature. H dropping is a feature of an enormous number of accents of English, and it is becoming more and more common. It can be heard in many regional accents of England and Wales.	If you *are* a natural H-dropper, you will need to focus on *replacing* those dropped H's, so go to the end of this section for how to put your H's in!

'Andy 'ints for dropping your H's

See It

This is what the words look like when you take those H's away:

'Arry   'Obson   'ad   'oliday   'Awaii

They now start with a vowel!

Feel It

Say these individual words, starting them with the vowel:

'Arry   'Obson   'ad   'oliday   'Awaii

'Ear it [TRACK 22 (as above)]

Listen again to the whole sentence. Notice how with the Cockney speaker the words are *linked* from one to the next.

Harry Hobson had a holiday in Hawaii

HOW TO DO ACCENTS

The speaker treats the H-dropped word *as if it never had an H*. The words flow together just as they would with any word that started with a vowel. Watch out: a common mistake is for people to replace the 'missing H' with a glottal stop. Wrong!

The other lovely detail is: words that in standard English grammar would have had the indefinite article *'a'* before them now have *'an'*, as in this example:

A holiday becomes An 'oliday

Not all H-dropped accents do this. It is worth noting that in many young contemporary London accents, for example, this flow is disappearing, leading to a much more choppy staccato quality in the speech.

Hear It [TRACK 23]

- Young Contemporary London:

·arry ·obson ad a ·oliday in Hawaii

TOP TIP ───

*H-droppers sometimes aren't sure if a word starts with an H or not! They may think they dropped an H, when in fact they didn't! This can lead to a comic phenomena known as **'hyper-correction'** when they put it an H which should never be there!*

Ask an H-dropper how to say the letter Aitch: they may well answer Haitch!

How to put H's back in

Although H-doers may drop an H from a word that has no stress or weight at all, they would *never* do this is the word is stressed. Take this sentence, for example: 'It was his first offence.' If the stress is put on the word **first** then the H on **his** may get dropped: 'It was 'is FIRST offence'. But if the stress is on the word **his**, that H comes striding back in again: 'It was HIS first offence'. If you are naturally an H-doer, you will follow this pattern too, but if you are not, getting that H to make an appearance may need a little concentration.

An H is just a puff of air, nothing more.

See It

In Shaw's *Pygmalion*, Henry Higgins teaches Eliza Doolittle to put her H's in by speaking in front of a candle flame. As she pushes out the puff of 'H', she can see the flame flicker. Not a bad technique: try it!

You could also use a mirror, or a pane of glass, and watch it steam up as you push the H puff of air onto it.

Feel It

- Put one hand on your stomach and the other in front of your mouth.
- Pant like a puppy. One hand will feel the muscles that do the pushing, the other will feel the warm air. That's an H!

Although this is pretty simple, it takes practice to drop this action into the midst of speech when you're not used to it.

- Try these phrases:

  I **h**ope so. I **h**ope you **h**ave.
  I **h**ope you **h**ave your **h**at.
  We **h**ave to. We **h**ave to **h**ide.
  We **h**ave to **h**ide in **h**ere.

TOP TIP ——————————————————————————

*Just because it's a strong regional accent, doesn't mean they H-drop. Don't make the mistake of H-dropping when you shouldn't. Scottish and Newcastle are **not** H-dropped accents, for example – dropping the H in these accents will give the game away! (That's why it's a Major Player...)*

The sentence below will quickly illustrate whether you and/or your speaker is an H dropper or not.

H: Harry Hobson had a holiday in Hawaii.

You and the New

Are you an H-doer or an H-dropper? What about your new accent? Make a note in the **You and the New** charts at the back of the book.

Spotlight on NG

What makes this a Major Player is...

NG's can be **Hard**, **Soft** or **Dropped**.

And *which* one you use *when* depends on what type of word it's found in!

The kinds of words in which NG is found fit into two groups with distinct rules:

Group A – 'NG' Words

- NG nouns (people, objects) – a **Gong**; a **Singer**.
- NG verbs (doing words) – to **Hang**; to **Bring**.
- NG adjectives (describing words) – **Long**, **Strong**.

The rule? These can be hard or soft, but *never* dropped.

Group B – 'ING' Words

- ING verb endings (continual doing words) – RUNNING; LAUGHING (For the smarty pants amongst you these can also be known as the 'present participle'!)

The rule? These can be hard or soft, and *frequently* dropped!

Hear It [TRACK 24]

Listen to the two NG possibilities, hard and soft, on these Group A Words:

> Gong   Singer   Hang   Bring   Long   Strong

- **Hard:** *Manchester*
  With hard NG's you will hear a G or K quality on the end of the word.
  (Found in accents of the Midlands and North West of England, and also in accents with a Slavic or Yiddish influence, for example.)
- **Soft:** *Essex*
  With soft NG's you *won't* hear a G or K.

(Found in all southern English accents and all North American accents, for example.)

Hear It [TRACK 25]

Group B words can also be both hard and soft as above, but they can also be **dropped**. Listen to these accent examples dropping the NG on the word running.

- **Dropped:** With dropped NG the action moves to the front of the tongue, making an N sound! But the fun doesn't stop there. Each accent will have its own specific sound that will fit one of the following styles:

  1 runn'N *Norfolk* (and Southern US States, Irish and Newcastle)

  2 runnEN *Wales* (and English South West and North West)

  3 runnIN *London* (South East England, Midlands, Yorkshire)

  4 runnEEN *Canadian* (Parts of Canada and America)

  Running   Laughing   Dancing

Make sure you get the right kind of **drop** for your authentic accent.

The Patterns

The great thing is that many accents will pick and mix. This result is **four** possible patterns across the A and B words:

1 **Hard** in A and B words

2 **Soft** in A and B words

3 **Hard** in A words and **dropped** in B words

4 **Soft** in A words and **dropped** in B words

Which combination do you use? Does your new accent use the same? If not, learn the new sound and practise the new pattern.

Learn the new sound

How to do a Hard NG

See It

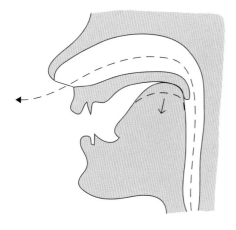

The back of the tongue is up on the soft palate.

It finishes with a squeeze that releases into the 'click' of a K or the 'bounce' of a G.

Feel It

Complete the NG with a K or a G on all the A and B examples in this sentence. (You'll see that A and B come together in the word **singing**!)

     A   A B   A   A B   B A

The singer was singing for the king. As she was singing and skipping along

       A   A   A   A

to the song, the king sang along too!

How to do a Soft NG

See It

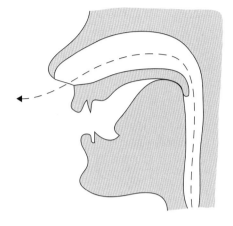

The back of the tongue is up on the palate and the sound goes into the nose.

The back of the tongue then has a soft release as it drops down silently.

If you are used to hard NG's then this will feel as if you haven't finished the sound!

Feel It

Use a soft NG on all the A and B examples in this sentence.

Make sure you don't squeeze, click or bounce!

A   A B   A   A B   B A
The singer was singing for the king. As she was singing and skipping along

A   A   A   A
to the song, the king sang along too!

NB: Accents that use soft NG in A and B words do in fact use hard NG-G but only in words such as:

- Longer, Stronger / Longest Strongest (comparative and superlative adjectives, adding an -er/est suffix to the basic adjective).
- Finger, Anger, Jungle (where the ending (-er or -le) is *not* a suffix, but is part of the structure of the word).

How to do a Dropped NG

See It

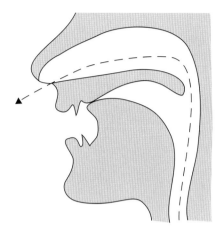

With dropped NG's the action of the tongue has shifted from the back to the front, effectively creating an N!

There are then two ways of dropping *into* the N:

Feel It

- IN – EN – EEN: There is an obvious vowel before the N and a clear second syllable.
- N: There is no vowel before the N. The syllables crunch together.

Try dropping your NG's in each of these ways, but remember: only on the Group B examples.

```
     A        A B       A              A B          B   A
The singer was singing for the king. As she was singing and skipping along
```

```
        A      A   A    A
to the song, the king sang along too!
```

For some speakers (but certainly not all) dropping on the Bs is optional, so that in more formal speech they will use whichever NG they use for the A words.

Practise the patterns:

Now you know how to do the sounds, practise the patterns!

1 **Hard** in A and B

2 **Soft** in A and B

3 **Hard** In A and **dropped** in B

4 **Soft** in A and **dropped** in B

The sentence below will quickly illustrate which NG pattern you and/or your speaker use.

ING: The singer was singing for the king.

You and the New

What do you do with your NG's? What about your new accent? Make a note in the **You and the New** chart at the back of the book.

Spotlight on TH

What makes this a Major Player is...

TH is a sound that accents love to have fun with. There are in fact *two* TH sounds in English, one made with voice and one without, and accents will treat them in different ways! Not only this, but they may do different things with them depending on whether they're at the beginning, middle or end of a word.

Hear It [TRACK 26]

Voiceless TH	Voiced TH
THick paTHetic broTH	THose broTHers baTHe
May be:	May be:
● **Standard TH**	● **Standard TH**
● **Plosive TH**	● **Plosive TH**
● **T substitute**	● **D substitute**
● **F substitute**	● **V substitute** (NB rarely used at the start of a word: 'ose brovvers not vose brovvers)

Just like many of the other sounds we've looked at, these will work in patterns. Here are the five most widespread patterns currently in operation in accents of English.

1 **Standard TH's** everywhere (Scottish, most American, standard varieties of English).

2 **Plosive TH's** everywhere (many Southern Irish accents).

3 **T/D Substitutes** – Changes to **T** and **D** everywhere (West Indian and *some* Southern Irish).

4 **Voiced TH** – Changes to **D** at the start of a word, but **V** in the middle and end. **Voiceless TH** – Changes to **F** everywhere. (Contemporary urban English.)

5 **Voiced TH** – **dropped** at the start of a word and **V** in the middle and end. **Voiceless TH** – changes to **F** everywhere. (Traditional London.)

Which of these TH patterns sounds most like your own? What is your new accent's pattern? You will need to know not only *how* to do its TH's but also *when*…

Hear It [TRACK 27]

Listen to the patterns in operation in these accents:

1 *Standard English (RP)*

2 *Southern Irish*   It's a **th**ick pa**th**etic bro**th**

3 *West Indies*

4 *Contemporary London*   Look at **th**ose bro**th**ers ba**the**

5 *Essex*

TOP TIP

*Although there are regional patterns in operation, they are constantly changing, and the pattern an individual speaker uses will be strongly affected by their generational and cultural influences. Listen to an example of your new accent to see what pattern **they** use. It may be one of the above or it may be a new one!*

Before you can do any of the patterns you will need to check you can physically make the sounds. Listen to the speakers on TRACK 27 to compare your new sound with theirs.

How to do the varieties of TH

1 Standard TH

 See It

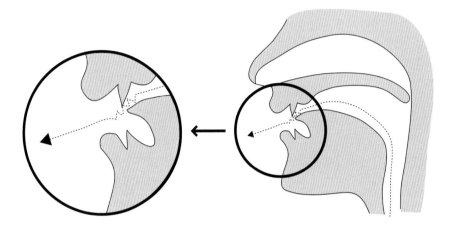

For the standard TH…
- The tongue almost touches the under side of all the top front teeth.
- The air is released with friction.
- Look in the mirror to see the tongue in position.

 Feel It
- Coat the underside of all the top front teeth *gently* with your tongue tip.
- Push air gently between the tongue and teeth and feel the air escaping. The tongue must stay soft to do this!

 Hear It
- Hear the air escaping with a hissing sound. That's the friction! That's your **standard voiceless TH**.
- Add voice to it and you have your **standard voiced TH.**

Now try using the standard TH on these sentences:

It's a **th**ick pa**th**etic bro**th**   Look at **th**ose bro**th**ers ba**th**e

HOW TO DO ACCENTS

2 Plosive TH

When the contact between two articulators is firm you will feel the trapped air explode as the two articulators spring apart, making the sound a 'plosive'.

See It

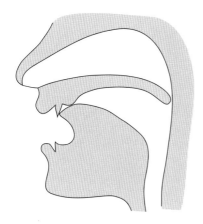

For the plosive TH the tongue is in *exactly the same position* as for standard TH, but the tongue is *pushed against* the teeth and the air is *not* released with friction, instead the tongue springs off the teeth, so now it's a plosive!

Look in the mirror to check the position of your tongue is the same as with standard TH.

Feel It

- Push the tongue onto the back and under side of your top teeth.
- Keep it spread wide, just like a standard TH.
- Push against the teeth and bounce away in a T-like manner.

Hear It

- The sound explodes, so you won't hear friction. That's your **voiceless plosive**.
- Add voice to it and you have a **voiced plosive**.

So, for the plosive TH the only thing that changes from standard is the way the sound is released. This gives it a T- or D-like quality, but it's definitely not a T or D!

Now try using the plosive TH on these sentences:

It's a **th**ick pa**th**etic bro**th**   Look at **th**ose bro**th**ers ba**th**e

3 T and D Substitutes

 See It

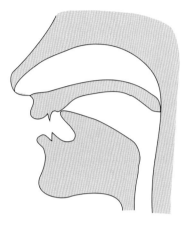

For T and D substitutes the tongue tip usually moves to the gum-ridge as in this illustration.

 Feel It

Replace all the TH's with T's in the first sentence and D's in the second, making them on your gum-ridge:

It's a **t**ick pa**t**etic bro**t**   Look at **d**ose bro**dd**ers ba**de**

4 F and V Substitute

 See It

For the F substitute simply make a pure old-fashioned F.

Look in the mirror to see the top teeth tickle the bottom lip.

HOW TO DO ACCENTS

Feel It

Replace all the TH's in the sentence with Fs.

It's a **f**ick pa**f**etic bro**ff**

There's a twist, however: accents that use the V substitution only use it in the middle and ends of words, not at the start. At the start they will either use a D substitute, or they will drop the sound completely!

Replace the TH's in this sentence with V, but drop the first one:

Look at **'**ose bro**vv**ers ba**v**e

In fact, if there's one accent that can illustrate this it has to be Cockney! Listen to this example:

Hear It [TRACK 28]

- That's right, Bethany's with your brother!   becomes
  'As, right, Beffany's wiv your bruvver!

The sentence below will quickly illustrate which TH pattern you and/or your speaker uses.

TH: That's my brother with a thermos of Matthew's broth.

You and the New

What happens to your THs? Do you need to learn new ones for your new accent? Make a note in the **You and the New** chart at the back of the book.

Major Issues

Consonants can be affected by these Major Issues:

- **Voice**, **Place** and **Manner** (how they are made).
- The **Glottal Stop** (where did that consonant go?).
- **Collisions** (dropping and crunching: when consonants collide).

The way in which accents play with consonants can differ enormously from one region to another. In some accents the consonants may be playful and soft; in others they may be sharp and precise. And as speech gets more rapid or informal they may disappear, merge together or even reappear as something else! *Junowo-ameen? Geddi?*

Spotlight on Voice, Place and Manner

The way in which you make your consonants may be completely different from the way they are made in another accent.

Hear It [TRACK 29]

Compare the *consonants* of these speakers from Liverpool and the Punjab and you'll hear what we mean!

Kate's taking me down town to a comedy gig.

Every time you make a consonant you make three decisions:

1 How much vocal vibration is in the sound (**Voice**).

2 Where in the mouth the contact is made (**Place**).

3 The way in which the sound is released (**Manner**).

Change one or more of these three elements and the quality of the consonant will change, which could move you from Liverpool to Bolton: – a distance of a mere 36 miles, but a world apart in terms of consonant qualities.

Voice: feeling the buzz

'Voicing' is a term used to describe the vocal vibrations present (or not!) in a consonant. (See 'Knowing your equipment', page 19.) Some accents, such as Irish, like to take voice *out* of many sounds, and some accents, such as Cornish, like to *add* it. The effect on the quality of the sound and the feel in the mouth is dramatic. Voiced sounds may feel soft, springy or firm, while voiceless sounds may feel hard, tense and sharp. Developing sensory awareness of the way sounds feel in the mouth makes doing accents a pleasure.

Feel It

If you *remove* voice from the consonants in this sentence:

> Good God, that dog has fleas!

..the effect will be something like this:

> Koot kot that tok hass fleass!

While if you *add* voice to this sentence:

> Some people say stop.

…the effect will be something like this:

> Zome beoble zay zdob!

Have a go. Which one is most like your accent? As you do this you may feel and hear other accents emerging. When there is no voice you may hear the quality of Southern Irish, or German. When there is more voice you may hear the quality of the far South West of England: Devon and Cornwall. They may not do it all the time, and it may only be with certain sounds, but take notice if an accent favours **adding** or **removing** as their preferred quality.

Hear It [TRACK 30]

- *Southern Irish:* Good God, that dog has fleas
- *Cornish:* Some people say stop

There are eight pairs of sounds in English which have a possible voiced (shown in **bold**) and voiceless (shown in *italic*) version. Listen out for these sounds and you'll get the most mileage out of this Major Issue.

The eight pairs are:

- **B** / *P* (Be / *Pea*)
- **D** / *T* (Do / *To*)
- **G** / *K* (Got / *Cot*)
- **V** / *F* (Vat / *Fat*)

- **TH** / *TH* (This'll / *Thistle*)
- **Z** / *S* (Zed / *Said*)
- **ZH** / *SH* (Measure / *Shone*)
- **DJ** / *TCH* (Gin / *Chin*)

Place: feeling the contact

When you say a T or D, where does your tongue tip go? Which part of the mouth does it hit? Does the tip touch the back of the top teeth? Or does it curl up to the gum-ridge? Or maybe it curls down and you feel the whole of the front of the tongue pushing against your teeth.

By changing the **place** where a sound is made, you can fundamentally change not only the way it sounds and feels, but also the whole muscular setting of your mouth. If the tongue is always having to curl up to the roof of the mouth or push forward onto the teeth, then over time, as we learn to speak, it will develop a specific shape in the mouth ready to move to this target. This then creates a muscular *setting* in the tongue. Try it on these sounds.

Feel It and See It

Look in the mirror as you say the following sentence in your own accent:

What a to-do to die today

Where does your tongue make contact to make the T and the D?

Now try these target points for your T and D. Look in the mirror as you do them. How do they compare?

- **Teeth**
  1 Bite your front teeth close together and push the tongue onto the teeth. (*Essex*)
- **Gum-ridge**
  2 Keep your teeth apart. Curl the tip up onto the centre of the gum-ridge and don't touch the teeth at all. (*RP*)
- **Behind the gum-ridge**
  3 Keep the teeth apart and curl the tip of the tongue up and back towards the roof of the mouth. (*Punjabi*)

As you move the tongue and change the target points in the mouth, you will begin to hear accents other than your own. Moving target points will

HOW TO DO ACCENTS

change the tonal quality. As the target points move back in the mouth the resonance of the sound will get lower. Make a T or a K and move it gradually further back in your mouth: you will hear the notes drop.

Hear It [TRACK 31]

● *Essex*, *Standard English* (RP) and *Punjabi*: **What a to-do to die today**

All that just from changing the **place** of your T and D! Any consonant can change its place in the mouth. The Liverpool K is way back on the uvula; in many Indian and Pakistani accents the L, N, T and D all curl way back behind the gum-ridge; and when many contemporary regional accents of England say the word **Death** the TH moves so far that it becomes an F.

> **TOP TIP**
>
> *Any accent you do will have its own set of target points that the tongue heads towards and its own muscular setting. The muscularity required may be very different from your own. Knowing where these targets are and how the tongue feels getting there will help you to anchor the muscular setting of your new accent.*

Manner: feeling the release

When you make a K does it feel as if it explodes firmly out of your mouth? Does it feel splashy? Or full of friction? And what about when you make a TH? The way in which a consonant is **released** from your mouth will make a huge difference to the quality of the sound and therefore your accent. When the contact between two articulators isn't fully made, air will squeeze through the gap, producing friction and making the sound a 'fricative'. When the contact is firm you will feel the trapped air explode as the two articulators spring apart, making the sound a 'plosive'. Add an extra puff of air at the end and you have 'aspiration'.

Hear It [TRACK 32]

Friction v Explosion

Listen to the *fricative* sounds the Liverpool speaker uses on the P, T and K compared to the plosive sounds of the speaker from just down the road in Manchester.

I **can't cook** a **pot**ato or a chi**ck**en

And compare the *fricative* Scottish TH to the *plosive* Southern Irish TH.

That's the thickest **th**ing

As for adding an extra puff of air, many English accents love to put aspiration on their explosive sounds, giving them a 'hi-hat cymbal' quality, as this Essex speaker demonstrates. On the other hand there are those accents that love to remove aspiration, making the sound a little more 'bass drum' as our Punjabi speaker does.

Hear It [TRACK 33]

- *Essex* and *Punjabi*: **K**ate's **t**aking me **d**own **t**own **t**o a **c**omedy **g**i**g**

From voice to place to manner, hi-hat cymbals, or big bass drums, changing the way your consonants are made; the amount of voice you use, where you place them, and how you release them, will dramatically change the way they *sound* and also the way they physically *feel* in your mouth.

> **TOP TIP**
>
> *Be careful: when consonants are different from our own there is a strong tendency to judge them, eg: 'Those are just sloppy, those are lazy, and those feel aggressive!'. That may be true for you, but it is **not** how the authentic speakers feel. Getting the feeling of the accent in your mouth will give you the physical experience of speakers of that accent, essential to sounding and **feeling** authentic.*

Spotlight on the Glottal Stop

This is a sound that you will all know and recognise when you hear it, though you may not have known it had a name! The word 'glottal' means 'made in the glottis (the area between the vocal folds)' and the word 'stop' refers to the stopping of the air-flow. The sound it makes is that of a tiny cough or grunt!

Hear It [TRACK 34]

A glottal stop!

The glottal stop is used in accents to:

- *replace* a T
- *accompany* a T, P or K
- *replace* an F or TH (but only if you're a cockney!)
- *replace* the word TO or THE.

Hear It [TRACK 35]

- *Norfolk:* Pit Matter Frenetic
- *Newcastle:* Butter Paper Biker
- *Cockney:* Arthur Afternoon

The glottal stop doesn't have an English letter to represent it, but it does have a phonetic symbol: **?** (Yes, it does look very like a question mark, as though it is asking 'Where's the sound gone?': this is a handy reminder that it is often a *substitute* for a missing sound.) We will use **?** whenever the glottal stop is being illustrated. 'Ge?i?'?

How to do a Glottal Stop

See It

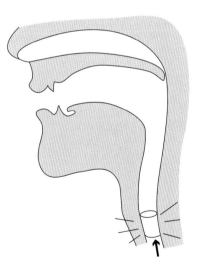

The sound is made in the **Glottis**, which is the space between the vocal folds. The tongue doesn't move *at all*. The vocal folds come together and STOP the air-flow momentarily. The air then 'pops' out when the folds open for the next sound, making a little grunt.

Feel It

- Open the mouth and let the tongue tip rest against the bottom teeth.
- Make a tiny single cough sound and feel the 'pop' of air in the throat. That's a glottal stop!

How to replace a T

Use the cough of a glottal stop to substitute the T in these words. Don't move that tongue to make a T, let it lie flat!

- On the ends:

    Pit = Pi?   Hat = Ha?   Cut = Cu?

- In the middle (before unstressed syllables only):

    Matter = Ma?er   Glottal = Glo?al
    Kitten =ki?en   Frenetic = Frene?ic

- In-between:

    Get off = Ge?off   Might as well = Migh?as well   What if = Wha?if

 Hear It [TRACK 36]

Listen to our Norfolk speaker saying all the above.

> **TOP TIP**
> *Even though you have taken the T out, make sure you are putting the energy of the missing sound into the glottal stop. Don't over-relax. It shouldn't feel soft!*

Speakers that substitute T with a glottal stop are often aware that they do it, and can choose to replace the T if they want or need to. London accents are *very* versatile in the way they use this feature. A glottal T is considered the norm, but they may put the T back for emphasis or extra clarity (though it always lags a little behind!).

How to do a glottal stop accompanying a T, P and K

This is a lovely feature of accents of the North East of England. In fact understanding and recreating the unique way they treat the T, P and

HOW TO DO ACCENTS

K collectively is *essential* if you want to have a believable North East accent.

Cockneys, East Anglians and some areas of Scotland such as Dundee and Kinross also do this, but they tone it down for the P and the K, using a full glottal replacement for the T.

In an *accompanying* glottal stop the tongue or lips only take up the *position* of the consonant P, T or K. The sound is *released* from the glottis.

See It

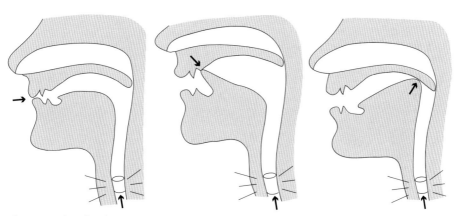

Accompanying glottal stop: P   Accompanying glottal stop: T   Accompanying glottal stop: K

Hear It [TRACK 37]

(This may be hard to hear at first, but what you are listening for from our Newcastle speaker is a little extra beat *before* the glottal: it happens as the tongue and lips take up their position.)

- **Bu**t**ter Pa**p**er Bi**k**er**

  He put the butter in paper and gave it to the biker

Feel It

- Go to say the word as if you are about to do the consonant.
- When you reach the position of the P, T or K, *freeze!*
- Hold the articulators in the P, T or K position but *swap your focus* to the throat and 'cough' the next syllable out.

Once you can do it slowly, try speeding up. This may well be a very new thing for your mouth to do, so don't rush it!

biker = bi?er   cooker= coo?er   baker = ba?er   talker = tal?er
paper = pa?er   wrapper = wra?er   copper = co?er

Once you feel confident, try using it in the sentence:

He put the butter in paper and gave it to the biker

How to replace an F or TH

Use the cough of a glottal stop instead of the F and the FT and the TH in these words. Don't move the lips or the tongue to make the F or the TH, let it lie flat!

Half in   Afternoon   Arthur

It's that simple: one challenge is believing it, and another is that it can make things difficult to understand. Treat it with caution!

How to replace the word **TO** or **THE**

In many accents of the North of England the glottal stop replaces the word THE, whilst in many accents of Scotland and the South of England it replaces the word TO.

Hear It [TRACK 38]

'He's gone *to the* shop' becomes…
- *Essex:* **'Es gone ? the shop** (replacing the word TO)
- *Yorkshire:* **He's gone tu? shop** (replacing the word THE)

This is often written in playscripts like this: 'He's gone t' shop', 'On t' sideboard' – the apostrophe indicates a missing THE.

Feel It

Try each because the effect and the feel is very different!
- **'Es gone ? the shop** (replace the word TO with a little glottal cough)
- **He's gone tu? shop** (it will feel as if you are saying the word TUT without the final T)

HOW TO DO ACCENTS

The glottal stop is on a bit of a roll in accents of English. It's spreading like wildfire, so that accents that never used to do it, or even frowned upon it, have picked it up and made it their own. Listen to all the different accent examples telling their stories on the accompanying CD (TRACKS 86–96) and we are sure you'll hear plenty of them.

Spotlight on Collisions

Consonants don't always stand alone in a word. Life isn't that simple. Consonants often collide or cluster in the English language: sometimes within a word as in 'a**ft**ernoon'; and sometimes when two words collide, as in 'goi**ng t**o'.

Accents often make life much simpler by *dropping* consonants out of the cluster (**elision**) or *crunching* the consonants in the cluster together (**assimilation**).

Hear It [TRACK 39]

Listen to all these examples of consonants getting dropped from consonant collisions.

Where have all the T's gone?

- I**t's** the be**st p**eople I mo**st** miss – Is a bess people I mohs miss

And what about this T and TH?

- Wha**t's** that – Waasa?

Where has this entire FT cluster gone?

- A**ft**ernoon – Ahʔernoon

Or this TH?

- He said something – **He said sommingk**

- She's going out with him – **She's going out wi yim**

And where are the L and R from this collision?

- Alright – **Awight**

As consonants collide they may even merge into one another, crunching together, sometimes changing one of the sounds, and sometimes making a completely new sound altogether. It happens to varying degrees in all accents, particularly as a result of rapid relaxed speech. If you say the phrase, 'How do you get to London Bridge?', it may surprise you to notice that many of you will actually be saying 'LondoM Bridge'. That is a consonant crunch! Accents may do crunches that your mouth wouldn't even dream of, and that's where the fun begins…

And here are some crunches for you to get your ears and mouth around. Look at how we've written the phrases, listen to the examples and then have a go yourself.

Hear It [TRACK 40]

- *Essex:* Goo**d G**od! Wha**t do y**ou want? – **Goog God. Wochoo wamp?**
- *Manchester:* You've lo**st y**our ha**ndb**ag – **You've losh-chor 'ambag**
- *Glasgow:* What are you going to do? – **Wayeegundee**

And here are some of the most widespread consonant crunches, demonstrated by our *West Midlands* speaker:

Hear It [TRACK 41]

- **DY:** Di**d y**ou do your **du**ty? (The DY crunches to J, as in Judge)
- **TY:** I'll pass that **tu**na over to you. (The TY crunches to CH)
- **STY:** I guesse**d y**ou were **st**upid. (The STY crunches to SH-CH)
- **DR:** I had a **dr**eam about **dr**uids. (The DR crunches to JR)
- **TR:** The **tr**ain ran out of pe**tr**ol. (The TR crunches to CHR)
- **STR:** The **str**eet was ex**tr**emely **str**aight. (The STR crunches to SH-CHR)

Dropping and crunching may eventually become the accepted norm for a word, and so no longer considered an accent feature (as demonstrated by the word **cupboard**!).

HOW TO DO ACCENTS

The 'T' sound

'T' seems to act as a magnet for *all* the Major Issues: knowing what to do with it can quickly give you the tongue setting for your accent.

You've heard it getting dropped and crunched in consonant collisions – now listen to what can happen to it in Cockney in this one simple sentence:

Hear It [TRACK 42]

There are three ways this speaker can say a T, depending on how he feels!

Pass the butter, Mum

- The first is an example of **glottal substitution**: buʔer
- The second is an example of **voicing**: budder
- The third is an example of **dental placement** and **aspiration**: buТТer

Crunching, dropping, voicing, glottalising, dentalising and aspiration are a key indicator of the setting: all this from one little sound! Now you can see, and hear, why overlooking the Major Issues could be a major mistake.

The Springing Consonants

There are three consonants of English that can be termed **Springing Consonants**. In springing consonants (also referred to as semi-vowels) the articulators move *towards* each other, don't actually touch, and then *spring* apart. They are W, R and Y.

Because of this special quality they are often given a special job when vowels collide! A lovely little detail in some accents is the need for the mouth to insert a springing consonant to 'spring' from one vowel to another.

Hear It [TRACK 43]

Listen to these three speakers saying the phrase: **How are you?**

- *Lancashire:* In this example you can hear a **W** being inserted to push out the word **are**.

How w-are you?

You may think it's because there's a W in the spelling, but how muscular do you make that W? And what about, 'No idea.'? There's no W in the spelling there, but still some accents really use the power of that W.

- *Cockney:* In this example you can hear an R being inserted.

Haa r-are you?

This may surprise you. But listen to the shape of the vowel being made in the word **How**. Because it is an open AA shape, the lips aren't ready for a W, instead this speaker prefers an R!

- *Belfast:* In this example you can hear a **Y** being inserted.

High y-are you?

Again, listen to the final shape of the vowel in the word **How**. It is close to an EE shape, so again the lips aren't ready for a W, so instead the tongue chooses a Y.

Each of these example accents finds the springing consonant (W, R or Y) that is *closest in shape* to the vowel they have just made, and uses this to spring into the next vowel.

> **TOP TIP**
>
> *Listen out for these springing consonants being used in any accent you are working on. They can add real authenticity to your sound and help you with the momentum and rhythm of the accent.*

YOO!

The springing consonant Y often makes a special appearance before the vowel OO! When this sound appears as a speech sound in an accent, we will call it 'YOO'. (It may also be referred to as the 'liquid YOO' or 'YOD'.)

Most accents still use this sound, but when they use it will all depend on spelling! Take the words **Cute** and **Coot**, for example. We bet you don't say

HOW TO DO ACCENTS

them the same way (unless you're from Norfolk, England!). And what about **Beauty** and **Booty**?

Hear It [TRACK 44]

Listen to the words in this sentence spoken in an older Upper Class RP accent, keeping all the Y-OO pronunciations (written in bold):

> Rather than be **le**wd, he pre**su**med it was his **du**ty to play a **fe**w **su**itable **cu**te **tu**nes **beau**tifully and with en**thu**siasm.

That's the sound!

Let's start with some absolutes. This sound would *never* be heard, *whatever* the accent…

- In words with O or double OO or OU in the spelling such as: **Move, Boot** and **Soup**.

- After an L that has another consonant before it: **Glue, Clue, Blue**.

- After an R: **Rude, True**.

- After CH or J sounds: **Chew, Juice**.

(I know we said whatever the accent…but Wales is an exception! Welsh speakers have a 'flexible' relationship with this sound. They have a version of their own that is closer to I-OO than YOO. The only time they *wouldn't* use it is in the **Move, Boot, Soup** words. All the others may have it, or the English YOO.)

It is in all the *other* spellings that the fun begins!

What happens to the all possible YOO's in this sentence when *you* read it in your own accent?

> Rather than be **le**wd, he pre**su**med it was his **du**ty to play a **fe**w **su**itable **cu**te **tu**nes **beau**tifully and with en**thu**siasm.

…the chances are that they don't *all* have the YOO sound in them.

> You are likely to be using one of the following patterns. You need to know which one pattern you use and which one your new accent uses:
>
> - YOO's everywhere.
> - YOO dropping after L and S.
> - Dropping after L and S and crunching after T and D.
> - YOO dropping after *all* gum-ridge consonants: S Z N T D L and TH's.

1: YOO's everywhere

The only speakers that use YOO's everywhere (with the spelling exceptions noted above) are older, upper class, RP speakers. This can make it a great 'period RP feature' for characters in Noël Coward plays and the like.

Here are just a few of the words you can have fun with in these accents:

> suitable   lewd   sexual   absolute   suicide

 Hear It [TRACK 44]***:***

- *Standard English (RP):*

    Rather than be **le**wd, he pre**su**med it was his **du**ty to play a **fe**w **su**itable **cu**te **tu**nes **beau**tifully and with en**thu**siasm.

2: YOO dropping after L and S

With the vast majority of contemporary middle-class English speakers the YOO has been lost after L's and S's. So all those lovely words above (**suitable**, **lewd**, **absolute**, **suicide**) no longer have YOO in these accents! (For reference, the OO sounds that were previously YOO are underlined.)

 Hear It [TRACK 45]

- *Yorkshire:*

    Rather than be <u>le</u>wd, he pre**su**med it was his **du**ty to play a **fe**w <u>su</u>itable **cu**te **tu**nes **beau**tifully and with en**thu**siasm.

    (NB: 'presumed' may look like it has an S in it, but it's said as a Z!)

This only applies to stressed syllables, however. The YOO *remains* after the L in unstressed syllables:

- VALue
- SALuTAtions

And changes to SHOO after the S in unstressed syllables:

- TISHoo (tissue)
- ISHoo (issue)

3: Dropping after L and S and crunching after T and D

If the regional accent is a little stronger, as well as dropping YOO after L and S, the vast majority of regional British accents will 'crunch' the YOO after a T D and Z so that **tune** becomes **choon** and **duty** becomes **jooty**, and **presumed** becomes **prezhoomed**. This is a bit of a social class give-away, so don't do it if your character is middle class!

Hear It [TRACK 46]

- *West Midlands*:

  Rather than be lewd, he presumed it was his duty to play a **fe**w suitable **cu**te tunes **beau**tifully and with en**thu**siasm.

4: YOO dropping after all gum-ridge consonants: S Z N T D L and TH's

This is the pattern used by the vast majority of North American accents. In those accents *none* of the following words has YOO in it.

- S: **suit** Z: **presume** N: **nude** T: **attitude** D: **duty**
  L: **lewd** TH: **enthuse**

Hear It [TRACK 47]

- *American*:

  Rather than be lewd, he presumed it was his duty to play a **fe**w suitable **cu**te tunes **beau**tifully and with en**thu**siasm.

At this point we need to make two special mentions.

The first concerns Wales. As we mentioned earlier, rather than inserting a Y before the OO, Welsh accents use a vowel close to I, making a sliding vowel sound I-OO. Listen to the way our Swansea speaker says the word **CURE** in her KIT LIST (TRACK 93) and you will hear this special sound. They may in fact use the English YOO in some words and the Welsh I-OO in others. Which sound they use when may depend on the age of the speaker, and whether there is a contrast being made between two words: for example, **Blue** has a pure OO vowel in Welsh English, but **Blew** has the I-OO slide.

Hear It [TRACK 48]

- *Welsh:*

  Rather than be lewd, he presumed it was his duty to play a few suitable cute tunes beautifully and with enthusiasm.

The second concerns Norfolk. In Norfolk they *never* use YOO except at the very start of a word like *uniform*! (British readers may be familiar with a well known Norfolk Turkey company with the advertising tag line 'They're bootiful!')

Hear It [TRACK 49]

- *Norwich:*

  Rather than be lewd, he presumed it was his duty to play a few suitable cute tunes beautifully and with enthusiasm.

(If anyone out there knows of any other accents with this pattern, please let us know!)

HOW TO DO ACCENTS

The Bite Checklist

Major Players

These are the sentences that will illustrate the Major Player patterns for you:

R: Margaret, Linda and Gerry asked Peter if Roland started with 'R'.

L: Larry the silly lamb slept peacefully in the field until hailstones fell.

H: Harry Hobson had a holiday in Hawaii.

NG: The singer was singing for the king.

TH: That's my brother with a thermos of Matthew's broth.

R

Taps, trills, molar, retroflex, soft or substitute?

Q: How is the R made?

Q: Where does it tap, bend, curl or bunch to?

Q: Which **zone** does it resonate in?

Q: How long does it last?

Q: Is it always the same R or does it depend on the sounds around it?

And remember, each accent will have its own special combination. It may be rhotic with a trill, or non-rhotic with a tap. What combination does your new accent use?

L

There are four L patterns: accents that use...

1 Only light L.

2 Only dark L.

3 Light and dark L combination.

4 Light L and W substitute combination.

Which one does your new accent use?

NG

Remember the Ng and ING words…

NG words: **Gong, Hang, Long, Strong, Singer.**

ING words: **Running, Laughing,** etc.

And the patterns…

   1   **Hard** in NG and ING words.

   2   **Soft** in NG and ING words.

   3   **Hard** in NG words and **dropped** in ING words.

   4   **Soft** in NG words and **dropped** in ING words.

Which combination does your new accent use?

TH

1 **Standard TH's** everywhere (Scottish, most American, standard varieties of English).

2 **Plosive TH's** everywhere (many Southern Irish accents).

3 **T/D substitutes** – Changes to **T and D** everywhere (West Indian and *some* Southern Irish).

4 **Voiced TH** – Changes to **D** at the start of a word, but **V** in the middle and end. **Voiceless TH** – Changes to **F** everywhere. (Contemporary urban English.)

5 **Voiced TH** – **dropped** at the start of a word and **V** in the middle and end. **Voiceless TH** – changes to **F** everywhere. (eg traditional London/Cockney.)

Is your new accent following one of the above patterns?

H

H-doers or H-droppers?

- Do they drop or not? (Remember, this is only significant on *stressed* words.)

- Don't drop H's in an accent that doesn't, and vice versa!

HOW TO DO ACCENTS

Major Issues

Voice Place Manner

Check the eight pairs of sounds for voicing in your new accent:

- **B / *P*** (Be / *Pea*)
- **TH / *TH*** (This'll / *Thistle*)
- **D / *T*** (Do / *To*)
- **Z / *S*** (Zed / *Said*)
- **G / *K*** (Got / *Cot*)
- **ZH / *SH*** (Measure / *Shone*)
- **V / *F*** (Vat / *Fat*)
- **DJ / *TCH*** (Gin / *Chin*)

And for **any** consonant that catches your ear as being different ask yourself…

- How much vocal vibration is in the sound?
- Where in the mouth is the contact made?
- In what way is the sound released?

And check the T – It almost always has issues!

The Glottal Stop

How does your new accent use the glottal stop?

- *Replace* a T.
- *Accompany* a T, P or K.
- *Replace* an F or TH.
- *Replace* the word TO or THE.

Collisions

Listen for any **dropping** or **crunching** when those consonants collide.

They will be most frequent in: unstressed syllables, fast speech and informal speech.

If *you* drop or crunch but your new accent *doesn't*, beware! Don't infect your new accent with your own accent features!

The Springing Consonants

Listen out for the springing consonants W, R, and Y being used in any accent you are working on. They can add real authenticity to your sound and help you with the momentum and rhythm of the accent. You are likely to be using one of the following patterns (remember those exceptions given above). You will need to know which one pattern you use and which one your new accent uses.

- YOO's everywhere.
- YOO dropping after L and S.
- Dropping after L and S and Crunching after T and D.
- YOO dropping after *all* gum-ridge consonants: S Z N T D L and TH's.

5

THE SHAPES

(Vowels)

IN THIS CHAPTER...

To do any accent authentically, making and using the right vowel shapes is a must. Learning the vowel shapes and sounds of another accent can take you straight to the heart of it.

Did you know that every accent has its own set of distinct vowel shapes? Some accents have only five vowel shapes, some 12, while others have as many as 19. (Note that this has nothing to do with written English. We may only write five vowels but we may say many more!)

You'd be amazed if you could see what is really going on in your mouth as you shape vowels: it sometimes bears almost no relation to what you think you are doing! We may be aware of what is happening with the front of the tongue, but there's much more to the tongue than meets the eye: the tip does all the delicate work and the root keeps the tongue in your mouth, but it's the body of the tongue that moves to shape your vowels.

Surprisingly large, tongues can morph into all sorts of shapes like a big lump of modelling clay. The hump of the tongue can rise up and flatten down. It can undulate, like a wave. It can freeze and be held at a particular spot. And the lips join in with this too, rounding and spreading in tandem with the tongue. That's how we make vowels.

Each accent has its own set of lip and tongue shapes and movements, and in your own accent your mouth can find them instantly without any 'thought'. That's what you spent your time doing when you were a baby: learning *your* accent's vowel shapes and movements. As a baby you dedicated hours to hearing the sounds around you, playing with the shape of your mouth, until the sounds *you* were making matched the sounds you were *hearing* and/or *seeing*. You then practised those shapes and movements over and over again until they became *locked* into your muscle memory. That's what babies do. That's how you learned to speak.

To do *new* accents your mouth will need to find and learn *new* shapes and movements and thus *new* sounds. Time to unlock your old muscle memories and create new ones.

Getting the Big Picture: Using a word list

People use vowels all the time, so you'd think it would be easy to hear what they are doing, but just when you notice one vowel, they've moved on to another and then another, and another! If you are trying to learn the new shapes, this can make life tricky. Hearing and mimicking words in isolation, however, enables the brain to calm down and focus on what it is hearing, seeing and feeling. This is where a word list comes in handy.

The phonetician J C Wells devised the following word list, known as the 'KIT LIST'.

1 KIT	7 NURSE	13 CLOTH	19 PRICE
2 DRESS	8 TRAP	14 THOUGHT	20 CHOICE
3 STRUT	9 BATH	15 NORTH	21 MOUTH
4 FOOT	10 PALM	16 FORCE	22 NEAR
5 GOOSE	11 START	17 FACE	23 SQUARE
6 FLEECE	12 LOT	18 GOAT	24 CURE

This word list can illuminate the three fundamental things you need to know about an accent's vowels: the **shape** they make, the **inventories** they have, and the way the vowels are **distributed**. (These terms are explained below.)

But before we get technical, why not let it speak for itself? Choose a reading of the KIT LIST at the start of each track from 86–96 that has a different accent from yours, or use your own resource recording if you have made one.

Hear It [CHOOSE A TRACK FROM 86 TO 96]

Listen to it once through. Do nothing, just listen!

Hear It and Feel It

Listen to it again, and this time mimic what you hear: just as with a language tape, repeat each word after you hear it. You might be surprised by what your brain absorbed from only hearing it twice!

Mimicking *accurately* requires good ear and mouth co-ordination. It is lots of fun for the brain to listen, absorb and copy. But be careful: the brain also likes to translate what it hears into sounds and movements it already knows!

Skip back to the start, listen and mimic again. This time listen not for what you *expect* to hear, but what you *really* hear! Pay particular attention to:

- Vowel shapes and sounds which are different from yours.
- Vowel shapes and sounds which are similar but not quite the same.
- Words that have unexpected vowel shapes and sounds.

Although you are focusing on shapes and sounds, this word list is in fact also giving you valuable information on the way your new accent organises its vowels, telling you how many vowels it uses and when. All this from 24 little words: magic!

Vowels: Inventories and Distribution

Sounds like a delivery service? Well, in a way, it is. In order to deliver your vowels to the right area, you'll need to know *how many* vowel packages you have and *where* they are going! (Be warned: this section can bamboozle when you first read it. Don't be alarmed! Read it as many times as you need. It's really quite straightforward, it's just the concepts that may be new.)

Inventories

An 'Inventory' is a list of the vowels used by an accent.

Every accent has its own 'vowel inventory', a list of vowel distinctions recognised and used by that accent. An inventory is not concerned with *how* those vowels are made, just whether they exist or not. An inventory is really a numbers game. Some accents have only five vowels, some 12, while others have as many as 19!

When you listen to the Scottish (Glasgow) reading of the KIT LIST (Track 89) you will hear only 12 vowel shapes being used, some with an R after them and some on their own, but still only 12 vowel shapes. Listen to the Standard English (RP) speaker (Track 96) on the other hand and you will hear 19 separate vowel shapes! Those are their **vowel inventories**.

 Hear It [TRACKS 89 AND 96]

Listen to these two example speakers reading the KIT LIST.

- Listen to how some of the Scots words use the same vowel: **FOOT** and **GOOSE** have the same vowel, **TRAP** has the same vowel as

HOW TO DO ACCENTS

BATH, PALM and START. LOT, CLOTH, THOUGHT, and NORTH all have the same vowel: quite different from the Standard English (RP) speaker.

- And listen to the last three words. Because Scottish is a rhotic accent these are made with one of the 12 vowels plus an R. NEAR uses the FLEECE vowel. SQUARE uses the DRESS vowel, CURE uses the FOOT vowel. For the Standard English speaker we hear three new sliding vowels.

Countries can be divided up into 'accent inventory' areas. Scotland has a different inventory from England. The North of England has a different inventory from the South. The East Coast of America has a different inventory from the West, and so on.

The important thing is to know and use each of the vowel shapes in your new accent's inventory and you can identify this by listening to the KIT LIST.

If an accent shares the same vowel inventory as you the only differences you will hear in their version of the KIT LIST will be the specific *shape, length* or *movement* of those vowels. It may surprise you to know, for example, that HM the Queen and the Cockney Pearly King have the same vowel inventories as each other: it is the shapes and sounds they make for each of those vowels that are obviously very different. So for the Queen to pass herself off as a Cockney she would need to work on those vowel shapes, lengths and movements (oh, and perhaps the foundations, a few major players and a bit of the groove too!).

If on the other hand an accent has a very *different* inventory from yours, you will notice even more striking differences. The Queen and the Cockney, not only have very different vowel shapes from a Scot, they also have a completely different inventory. They would have to lose a lot of their old vowel shapes, find a lot of very new ones and be careful not to let their old vowels slip back in!

Main Inventory issues

Let's cut to the chase. When you listen to the KIT LIST these are the most significant 'inventory issues' you will need to listen out for and get right in your new accent:

- **STRUT – FOOT**: One vowel or two?

  Southern English accents have two different vowels for these two words, but Northern English accents only have one, making these words rhyme.

- **FOOT – GOOSE – MOUTH**: One, two, or three vowels?

  Accents in England, Southern Ireland and America have three different vowels, one for each word. Scottish and some Northern Irish only have two, one for **FOOT** and **GOOSE** but a different one for **MOUTH**. Some Scots only have one vowel, making them all rhyme!

- **LOT – THOUGHT**: One vowel or two?

  Canadians, Scots and some Americans have one vowel for these two words, where other accents have two.

- **PRICE – CHOICE**: One vowel or two?

  For most accents these are two very different vowels, but for some rural English, West Indies, Irish and Newfoundland accents they are the same.

- **NURSE – START – NORTH – FORCE – NEAR – SQUARE – CURE**
  (All the words with R)

  For rhotic accents, note the vowel that *precedes* the R (eg **START** takes the **TRAP** vowel in our Southern Irish example, TRACK 88). For non-rhotic accents, note the vowel that *replaces* the R (eg **NORTH** takes the **THOUGHT** vowel in our Standard English example, TRACK 96).

Distribution

'Distribution': which vowels go in which words?

Once you are familiar with the set of shapes the new accent has at its disposal, the next trick is knowing which vowel to put in which word. This can be tricky. After all, if two words have the same vowel in *your* accent you may well expect them to in your new accent, but you can't be so sure! An American actress was doing a great 'Noël Coward' English accent in *Private Lives*, until she came to the line, 'I'm all damp from the bath.' She confidently announced, 'I'm all dAHmp from the bAHth'. It was a lovely

English vowel shape, but little did she know that it belonged in **Bath**, but *not* in Damp. The Americans in the audience may not have noticed, but the English certainly did.

When it comes to knowing which vowel goes where, the 24 words on the KIT LIST are in fact more helpful than they look! Each word on the list represents a *whole set of words* that because of their spelling (and some history) will more than likely have the same vowel in it. For example, whatever vowel an accent uses for the word **CLOTH** it will also use for every other word in that group, such as **OFF** and **BOSS**; whatever vowel it uses in the word **STRUT** it will also use for **MOTHER** and **ENOUGH**. (We have provided lists of words found in each set with the KIT LIST on the *How to Do Accents* website, at www.howtodoaccents/kitlistsets. This is an invaluable resource. Though it is not an exhaustive list you will see patterns emerge in each group.)

Main Distribution Issues

And here's how to cut to the chase with distribution issues. When you listen to the KIT LIST listen to these words carefully. It is these sets of words that will have the most significant 'distribution issues' to watch out for in your new accent:

● TRAP – BATH – PALM – START

Northern English speakers, for example, will use a short 'a' in **TRAP** words and **BATH** words, but a long 'ah' in **PALM** and **START** words (the vowel is lengthened to reflect the L and R in the spelling).

Southern English speakers on the other hand only have a short 'a' in **TRAP** words. All the others have a long 'ah'.

Rhotic speakers may have all sorts of variations for **TRAP**, **BATH** and **PALM**, but they pronounce the R in the **START** words which can seriously affect the preceding vowel!

- **LOT – CLOTH – THOUGHT – NORTH**

  New Yorkers, Older London and upper class English speakers have a short 'o' in the **LOT** words, but a long, rounded 'aw' in all the others.

  Most other English speakers on the other hand, have a short 'o' in **LOT** and **CLOTH** words and a longer 'aw' sound in **THOUGHT** and **NORTH**.

  And of course rhotic speakers may have one vowel in **LOT**, another in **CLOTH** and **THOUGHT** and yet another followed by an R in **NORTH** words.

- **NURSE**

  Nurse words are a special category all of their own. They are derived from words with many different spellings:

  - **BIRD NERVE HEARD FUR WORD**

  Historically this indicates that they were once pronounced differently, but over time they have merged into one sound. What is significant is that in Scotland and Ireland (both rhotic accents) the merger wasn't complete! Some speakers still distinguish the vowels in these words, using their **DRESS** vowel before the R in **NERVE** and **HEARD**, but their **STRUT** vowel for **BIRD**, **FUR** and **WORD**, for example.

It is worth pointing out that individual word pronunciation does fluctuate over time, and is affected by peer groups, social aspiration, etc. This can make words move from one set to another over time. For example, Standard English *used* to put all its **'trans'** words (translate, transport, transaction etc) in the **BATH, PALM, START** sets with a long AH, but in recent times you will hear many speakers using the short **TRAP** vowel instead.

TOP TIP

*Once you know how a person says **one word** from the KIT LIST, the likelihood is they will say **all** the words from that group with the **same vowel sound**! This gives you invaluable information on the two basic structural issues around vowels: the Inventories **and** the Distribution.*

HOW TO DO ACCENTS

Getting more detailed: Environmental issues

So that's the **Big Picture**. Through using the KIT LIST you can gather the fundamental information you need on the shapes an accent uses, the distinctions it makes, and the way the vowels are distributed. Those are the basic essentials. But of course, in real life people don't simply read a list of words of your choosing, do they? (Shame!) They tend to speak in sentences, with words that aren't on your list and vowels surrounded by completely different consonants! Then what happens? Do those vowels behave differently in different 'environments'? A vowel is just like you; after all, you're a different person when surrounded by palm trees from when you're surrounded by concrete, and vowels are the same. They often behave very differently depending on the consonants around them, and whether the vowel is stressed or not.

There are five major environmental issues facing vowels, and none of them is global warming! They are:

- **Nasal Colouring** (see below)
- **R Colouring** (see page 122)
- **The L Effect** (see page 123)
- **Free or Blocked?** (see page 123)
- **Stressed or Unstressed?** (see page 124).

Nasal Colouring

One of the things you *might* have been hearing as you listened to the KIT LIST is **nasal colouring**: a vowel being 'coloured' by nasality. It happens in many accents when the vowel is in the environment of N, M or NG. As the soft palate drops to prepare for the nasal consonant the poor wee vowel gets caught on the wave and disappears down the nose.

Hear It [TRACK 50]

The most common occurrence of nasal colouring happens when the vowel is followed by N. As the tongue rises to the gum-ridge and the soft palate lowers, then off down the nose goes that vowel. You will also hear the whole *shape* of the vowel change as the N dominates it.
- *Essex/US:* Bee – Bean   Pat – Pant   Boat – Bone

Some accents love nasality so much they do it all the time, and they do it with extra whammy near an N, M or NG. Listen to the Manchester accent example on the CD (TRACK 91). This is an accent that uses **Nasal Spill**. This sounds disgusting but it's really not – it just means that the soft palate is held low *throughout* speech as part of the basic setting, so that sound continually 'spills' behind and down the nose.

Some accents use nasal spill on particular vowel shapes, especially the **PRIZE**, **TRAP** and **MOUTH** vowels, so clearly in order to do accents you need to have a flexible soft palate! (If yours is a bit sluggish have a look at 'Soft Palate' in 'Knowing your Equipment', page 23, for some basic exercises. If you need to do more work check out a good voice book such as the ones recommended in the Appendix, page 223.)

R Colouring

R colouring is a feature that will make your rhotic accents more detailed and authentic. It can be key to accents with strong molar and retroflex R's (see 'Spotlight on R', page 61) and it can really help you to distinguish one rhotic accent from another. It happens when a vowel is followed by an R. If the R is really strong, as the tongue moves to make it the vowel gets pulled along and 'coloured' by it.

R colouring is a feature of Northern Irish and many American accents, but it is not a feature of Southern Irish or Scottish. In these accents the vowel is said 'cleanly' and distinctly from the R that follows it.

Hear It [TRACK 51]

> Listen to the two speakers (*Southern Irish / American*) saying the words: I heard the car.
> - The *Southern Irish* speaker says the vowels *cleanly* and then *follows* them with the R.
> - The *American* speaker starts moving to the R *immediately after the H and C* so that it swallows or dominates the vowels.
>
> That's R colouring!

Vowels may be affected to different degrees in different accents. With the ER sound, as in **HEARD**, **BIRD**, etc, the R often replaces the vowel completely, whereas with other vowel + R combinations it may simply alter the shape of the vowel and pull back its resonance.

The L Effect

When a vowel is followed by a dark L or a W Substitute (see 'Spotlight on L', page 71), the whole shape may change. The back of the tongue rises up for the L and the vowel shape sometimes goes with it! Older RP speakers have the same vowel for **GOAT** and **GOAL** but younger speakers don't, and the London **FACE** vowel is completely different from the London **FAIL**.

Hear It [TRACK 52]

Compare the vowels in **pale** to **faced**, **goat** to **goal**, and listen to the 'e' in **felt** to **unwell**, in these three accents. That's the L effect!

- *Old RP / New RP / London:*
  The goat in goal was pale-faced and felt unwell!

(And in the Cotswolds '-el' words (**Well**, **Elf**, etc) are pronounced 'OW'!)

Free or Blocked?

Vowels often change if they're left free to hang out, or stopped gently by a voiced consonant, or pulled up short by a voiceless consonant. Compare your vowel in these words:

  May   Made   Mate

Are they all the same shape? Are they all the same length?

There are so many examples of this, and often it is just a matter of length, but Canadians take it to another level! Compare the shape of their vowel in **High** to their vowel in **Height**, and what about their infamous **Out** and **About**? You might think this is just their **MOUTH** vowel, but compare the shape when they say **Now** and spot the difference. Do the **Out** vowel in a **Now** word and our Canadian friends will have a giggle at your expense!

Hear It [TRACK 53]

Compare **out** to **now** and **night** to **sky** in this example:

  Go out now and look at the night sky.

TOP TIP

*Vowels are **most** affected by the consonant that comes **next** in the word and these are the consonants that have the most impact:*

  L: GO – GOLD   N: PRAT – PRANCE   R: MAT – MARRY

Stressed or Unstressed?

Once you make a word with more than one syllable you then have other vowel decisions to make: which vowels to stress and which to leave unstressed. Vowels in *stressed* positions tend to keep their pure shape, but when they are *not stressed* it's a different story. Accents may do very different things with their unstressed syllables: they may keep the vowel shape pure, which gives the syllable a little extra weight, or they may drop the vowel completely and replace it with a **KIT** vowel, a **DRESS** vowel or, the most common choice, a little sound called a **Schwa**.

> **Schwa** is the name for a completely unformed vowel, made when the mouth relaxes. Because we have more unstressed vowels than stressed, this little sound is the most frequently heard vowel sound in the English language!

Hear It [TRACK 54]

    Comma   Edda   Letter

- *Liverpool:* Comm-E   Edd-E   Lett-E
- *Standard English (RP):* Comm-UH   Edd-UH   Lett-UH
- *Cockney:* Comm-AH   Edd-AH   Lett-AH

Hear It [TRACK 55]

Listen to these examples of different stress patterns causing different vowel shapes to appear:

- *Northern v Southern English:* **Contain Concern Condition**
- *English v American:* **Mobile Futile Fragile**

Unstressed word endings may only be small but you will need to know which vowel your new accent uses for each of these:

- HAPP**Y**: do they use the **KIT**, **DRESS** or **FLEECE** vowel shape? Southern English uses the vowel shape from **FLEECE**, but Lancashire may use **DRESS**, while Yorkshire uses **KIT**.

- LETT**ER**: Is there an R? If not, is it the same as Comm**A**?

- HORS**ES**: Is it a **KIT** or an un-formed schwa?

- COMM**A**: What is the final shape? Round? Spread?

HOW TO DO ACCENTS

There are many more examples of unstressed syllables. English is full of them. Suffice to say, listen out for those unstressed syllables to keep building a really detailed accent!

The extended word list

The extended word list overleaf contains words designed to isolate the more detailed information on how the vowels and consonants might behave in different combinations and environments. It is by no means definitive, but it is a huge help in highlighting more detailed information for you.

If you only have this list recorded you can pick out the KIT LIST words from it (written in italics) to listen for the basic Inventory and Distribution issues before listening to the full list for the more detailed Environmental issues.

It will also give you information on the Major Players, the Foundations and the neutral tune.

1 *KIT*	18 *GIRL*	35 TUESDAY	52 BEER
2 *DRESS*	19 BIRTH	36 *NORTH*	53 *SQUARE*
3 HEAD	20 BERTH	37 *FORCE*	54 HAPPY
4 NEVER	21 FLEE	38 POOR	55 LETTER
5 *TRAP*	22 FLEAS	39 *CURE*	56 HORSES
6 *CLOTH*	23 *FLEECE*	40 *THOUGHT*	57 COMMA
7 *LOT*	24 MEAT	41 MORE	58 WHICH
8 ONE	25 FACE	42 PAW	59 WITCH
9 *STRUT*	26 FAIL	43 *CHOICE*	60 SING
10 *FOOT*	27 STAY	44 *PRICE*	61 SINGING
11 BOOK	28 EIGHTY	45 PRIZE	62 GOING
12 *BATH*	29 *GOAT*	46 FIRE	63 NOTHING
13 FATHER	30 GOAL	47 *MOUTH*	64 BEETLE
14 DANCE	31 GHOUL	48 SHOUT	65 WITH
15 *PALM*	32 *GOOSE*	49 NOW	66 US
16 *START*	33 THREW	50 POWER	67 NEITHER
17 *NURSE*	34 NEW	51 *NEAR*	68 EITHER

You and the New

- Inventories and Distribution:

  Get to know your *own* vowel distinctions! You only need to do this once and it provides you with a yardstick against which you can compare any new accents.

  Make a note of how your accent handles the Main Inventory Issues and the Main Distribution Issues given above and compare all your new accents to it.

  If you want to be more thorough you can record *yourself* reading the KIT LIST, play it back and listen to it word by word, starting with KIT, and compare *all* the words on the list to it, ie: **KIT – DRESS / KIT – TRAP / KIT – LOT**, etc. Listen for any words that share the same vowel sound and shape. If none are the same, then **KIT** stands alone as a 'distinct vowel' shape, but if a word does have the same vowel shape then it belongs in the same set as **KIT**.

  (This may sound like it takes time, but in fact it doesn't: the list quickly gets shorter and shorter!)

- Environmental issues:

  Use a recording of free speech or the extended word list to identify how your new accent is affected by these environmental issues and compare it with your own:

  - Nasal Colouring.

  - R Colouring.

  - L Effect.

  - Free or Blocked.

  - Stressed or Unstressed.

  So, don't give your new accent nasal colouring if it doesn't use it, and be sure to get those unstressed syllables in shape.

5 THE SHAPES

Shape, Length and Movement

Using the word list you can identify vowels changing from your own accent to your new accent, but can you tell in what *way* they changed? And can your mouth reproduce those new sounds accurately? If you are lucky your ear and mouth will co-ordinate easily: your ear will hear the differences and your mouth will make the correct changes to the shapes. However, they are just as likely *not* to! There may be sounds that are unusual to your ear and your mouth may simply not know what to do.

To make life easier for your ear and mouth it helps to narrow down what kind of changes you might be hearing and feeling. Accents distinguish one vowel from another through differences in shape, length or movement:

- **Shape** – Jaw? Tongue? Lips? How open is the jaw? What is the tongue doing? How round or spread are the lips?

- **Length** – Is it longer or shorter than your vowel?

- **Movement** – Are the jaw, tongue and lip shapes fixed, or do they move? If they move, how much, and from where to where?

Hear It [TRACK 56]

Listen to these two people saying the word **GOAT** and read our descriptions of each, they are very different! Listen to them as many times as you like, and then try them!

Scottish: **GOAT**
- **Shape:**
  Jaw: Quite close together.
  Tongue: High at the back.
  Lips: Very round.
- **Length:**
  Fairly short/sudden.
- **Movement:**
  Held steady.

West Midlands: **GOAT**
- **Shape:**
  Jaw: Open at first then closing.
  Tongue: Starts flat, and then rises a little in the middle.
  Lips: Start relaxed then round.
- **Length:**
  Medium.
- **Movement:**
  Lots! Starts like A and ends like OO!

The Scot will have to make big changes to get that West Midlands sound and vice versa.

HOW TO DO ACCENTS

Feel It, See It, Hear It (CHOOSE FROM TRACKS 86 TO 96)

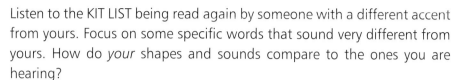

Now it's your turn.

Listen to the KIT LIST being read again by someone with a different accent from yours. Focus on some specific words that sound very different from yours. How do *your* shapes and sounds compare to the ones you are hearing?

Take one word at a time and repeat it first your way, then the new way, then your way, then the new way, etc, noticing the changes that you make each time. Look in the mirror!

Ask yourself:

Shape

- Is your jaw more open or closed for the new sound?
- What is the tongue doing?
- Are you lips more rounded or spread?

Length

- Is it longer or shorter? Does it glide away or snap off?

Movement

- Is the shape fixed or is it moving?

Okay…so we expect some of you are saying, 'What are they on about? I have *no* idea what my tongue is doing!' Believe us, you're not the only ones: it can be very hard to know what's going on in that mysterious black hole, and to work out exactly how you are making those sounds!

So let's start exploring shapes and making reference points to shine a light and give you a clearer view of the shapes of those vowels.

Making new shapes

Open your mouth into *any* shape, let your voice come through it, and you've made a vowel. Change the shape (by changing the position of the tongue, lips and jaw) and you change the vowel. Try it. Compare the shape of your **GOOSE** vowel to the shape of your **FLEECE** vowel. They are completely different.

When it comes to making your own vowel shapes you don't have to think about what your jaw, lips and tongue are doing. The shapes and sounds are firmly fixed in your muscle memory, your mouth has learnt them and it knows what it's doing even if you don't! But there are many more vowel possibilities than the few that your mouth is familiar with. Finding these *new* vowels may mean exploring new areas of the mouth and co-ordinating your tongue and lips in ways they have never tried before.

Remember, there are just three things that shape a vowel:

- **Jaw**
- **Lips (and Cheeks)**
- **Tongue**

It is the *combined position* of these three articulators that makes each vowel shape unique.

Through teaching your articulators the **neutral setting** of the jaw, lips and tongue, and then the most **extreme** vowel shapes and sounds possible, you can provide your ear and mouth with a clearer sense of geography and give yourself new reference points when listening to and learning the vowels of other accents.

When the mouth is in a **neutral setting** the sound it produces is a **neutral schwa** (not your accent schwa, which may be far from neutral: see 'Setting', page 41). And it is represented by the symbol **ə**. It is produced from a relaxed jaw and un-rounded lips with the tip of the tongue gently resting against the bottom front teeth.

Finding neutral schwa

Feel It

- **Jaw:** The jaw is released, but not open. This will mean that the back teeth are not touching, and the front teeth are apart, but not far enough for even your little finger to get in!
- **Tongue:** The tongue is lying flat in the bottom jaw, so that the slight hump in the middle of the tongue lines up with the centre point of the roof of your mouth. The tip of the tongue will just touch the back of the bottom teeth.
- **Lips:** The lips are neither round nor spread and the cheeks are soft.

See It

Look in the mirror to check that all your muscles are relaxed and that the teeth are just a fraction apart.

HOW TO DO ACCENTS

Hear It [TRACK 57]

Listen to the sound your mouth makes in this position. Add a little H before it, but don't change your mouth shape.

Now listen to us make this small, apparently insignificant, neutral schwa, as the unstressed vowel in the following words:

Comm**A**   Edd**A**   **A**bove   th**E**

If yours was noticeably different you may need to neutralise your setting a little more.

Now you know where the neutral centre is we can anchor eight extreme vowel shapes and sounds in your mouth.

Finding eight extreme vowels

This will give your ear and mouth eight new reference points, radiating out from the neutral schwa in the centre, like this:

See It

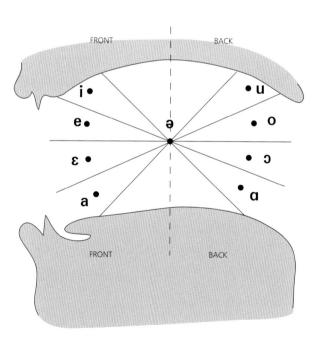

There are four reference vowels at the front of the mouth and four at the back, each labelled with a specific phonetic symbol.

When the body of the tongue makes a hump in the extreme point in each of these segments an 'extreme vowel' is heard. These sounds are also referred to as *cardinal* vowels.

Hear It and Feel It [TRACK 58]

Listen to us make each of the eight extreme vowel shapes, four at the front of the mouth and four at the back. Copy each sound as you hear it. (There is a more detailed step by step explanation of these shapes and sounds in 'Space Exploration' in the Appendix, page 214.)

You will hear them in this order: **i e ɛ a ɑ ɔ o u**

Front	Back
i	**u**
e	**o**
ɛ	**ɔ**
a	**ɑ**

See It

Jaw: During this sequence of vowels, what you can *see* on the outside is that the jaw moves from being close together for **i** to very open for **ɑ** then close together again for **u**.

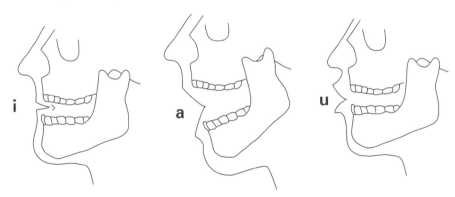

HOW TO DO ACCENTS

Lips: You can also see on the outside that the **lips** move from being spread for i, through to neutral for ɑ, then round for ɔ, o and u.

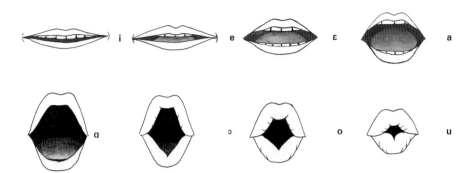

Tongue: What you *can't* see is that the **tongue**-hump starts high at the front of the mouth for **i**, flattens out for **ɑ,** then lifts high at the back for **u**. This picture gives you an impression of just what the tongue is doing through this sequence:

Hear It and Feel It [TRACK 59]

Listen as we make each of the shapes on a whisper. This way you hear the pure sound that the shape of your mouth is making, without the sound of your voice distracting you.

Front	Back
i	**u**
e	**o**
ɛ	**ɔ**
a	**ɑ**

Listen again and repeat each sound after us on a whisper so that you can really feel what your tongue is doing. It can help to close your eyes to use your mind's eye to picture the tongue shapes.

Hear It

Use your funnel (described in 'How to use this book', page 14) to listen to the sound of these whispered shapes.

See It

As you make the sounds, it is important to visualise the *shape* of your tongue and connect the *feeling* of that shape with the *sound* you hear.

Look in the mirror to see the position and shape of your lips, jaw and, where possible, your tongue.

TOP TIP

Watch out. Be precise. The brain is very good at translating what it hears into a sound or shape it already knows and making that sound and shape instead – don't let it!

The result of all this co-ordinated jaw, lip and tongue movement is that the sound frequencies on this sequence go from very high and bright for the **i**, through the middle of the spectrum for **ɑ**, to very low and dark for **u**! It looks a bit like this…

| i | e | ɛ | a | ɑ | ɔ | o | u |

Now you have eight extreme reference points in your ear and mouth, shining a light into the darkness, giving yourself a sense of the geography and location of vowels in your mouth. This has developed your ear–mouth co-ordination, opening up many more vowel possibilities than the few that your mouth was accustomed to.

Once your ear and mouth are familiar with these eight extreme vowels you can begin playing with the effects of lip-rounding: adding or removing lip-rounding to each of the tongue shapes to give yourself even *more* vowel possibilities. The more vowel possibilities you have available to you, the more accents you can do.

Playing with lip-rounding

Feel It

Adding lip-rounding
- Make the *inside tongue* shape of **i. Fix it in place** and add the *outside lip shape* of **u.** (This will make the Scottish vowel in the word GOOSE.)
- Make the *inside tongue* shape of **ɛ. Fix it in place** and add the outside lip shape of **u.** (This will make the Welsh vowel in the word NURSE.)

Removing lip-rounding
- Make the *inside tongue* shape of **ɔ. Fix it in place** and remove the lip-rounding to create the outside lip shape of **a.** (This will make the Leeds vowel in the word THOUGHT.)
- Make the *inside tongue* shape for the centre point **ə. Fix it in place** and add lip-rounding to it. (This will make a Yorkshire 'hesitation' sound or accent schwa in **commA.**)

Hear It [TRACK 60]

Listen to us as we do the above.

Application to Accents

As the hump in the body of the tongue undulates through the mouth it does not, of course, pass through solid lines that divide one sound from another. It works rather more like a rainbow. Where two areas meet, the sounds blend from one to another, providing a spectrum of vowels. A vowel may be halfway between **ɑ** and **ɔ**, for example: it may be on the borders, sharing qualities of both, it may move closer to the centre point or the extreme point, but you can only really know this when you: A) know what the extreme points are; B) know what they feel like; and C) know how they sound.

Here's what we mean: the vowel in the word **KIT**, for example, is made in the *general* area of the extreme vowel **i**, but specific accents may place it either very close to the extreme point or closer to the centre. The Glaswegian, New Zealand and Northern Irish **KIT** vowels (as in **'fish and chips'**) are good examples of this. In all of these accents the hump in the tongue is very close to the centre point and as a result the sound has some of the quality of ə.

Hear It [TRACK 61] *and See It*

Listen to these accent vowels and see where we have placed them in the spectrum. (The symbols we are using are the recognised phonetic symbols of the International Phonetic Association, or IPA.)

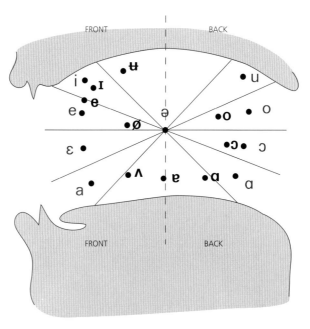

- The neutral centre point: ə
- *Cockney*: ʌ in STRUT
- *Glasgow*: ʉ in GOOSE
- *West Midlands*: ɪ in KIT
- *Manchester*: ɐ in PALM
- *Newcastle*: o in GOAT
- *Welsh*: ø in NURSE
- *Southern Irish*: e in FACE
- *Standard English (RP)*: ɔ in THOUGHT
- *Standard American*: ɑ in LOT

So here's the scoop...

Now when you hear a vowel sound you can think about it this way:

- What *area* in the vowel spectrum does it *sound* like it is focused in?
- What *extreme vowel shape* does it *feel* most like?
- Is it on the way to *another* extreme vowel shape? Is it close to the centre?
- Where does it belong on the spectrum?
- Are the lips rounded, relaxed or spread? (Remember how powerful lip-rounding can be.)

TOP TIP

*Remember your **Foundations** (page 33)? Get the foundations right and many of the simpler vowels will fall into place, leaving you free to focus on the tricky ones!*

So **shape** clearly matters...but what about **length**?

Length

The second way in which accents distinguish one vowel from another is through **length**. Within the list of vowel distinctions in an accent there may be some that are short and some that are long. Two vowels may be extremely close on the spectrum, but if the length is different it will be this that distinguishes them.

For some accents the **length of time** spent in one vowel shape is *crucial* while other accents aren't that bothered! New Yorkers are much fussier about their vowel lengths than many other North Americans, for example, and have strong distinctions between *long* and *short* vowels. Many Scots, on the other hand, prefer all their vowels to be short to mid length, taking the traditionally long EE (**FLEECE**) and OO (**GOOSE**) from South of the Border and shortening them, and conversely taking the shorter **DRESS** vowel and adding length to it – thus ironing out length distinctions.

> *Edda was working with a Canadian actor, playing a New York cop. His accent was great, he'd dealt with his 'oot and aboot', but when his character had to shout for the 'Doc' he headed back to Canada faster than a bullet from his gun! You see, Canadians love to lean into this 'Doc' vowel, keeping it long and steady, but New York cops are in a hurry, they use a short snappy vowel. He got the **shape** okay, but he just couldn't help using the Canadian **length**!*

 Hear It [TRACK 62]

Listen to:
- The short vowels of the *Scottish* speaker.
- The steady mid length vowels of the *Canadian* speaker.
- The long vowels of the *Norfolk* speaker.
- The switch from long to short vowels in the *Yorkshire* speaker.

   Move that dog's poop off the grass, please.

A vowel may be short and snappy, long and generous, or somewhere in between. The vowel lengths have a profound effect on the rhythm and pace of an accent: it's always worth remembering the influence of geography, climate, culture, etc, on the rhythms and music of an accent. Of course, emotional intention can also affect vowel length. Accents that group vowels into long and short distinctions may make their long vowels even longer and their short vowels even snappier when the word is strongly stressed. And don't forget, the vowel lengths may be being affected by those surrounding consonants.

Movement: Steady or Sliding?

The third and final way that accents distinguish one vowel from another is by keeping some **steady** and making others **slide**. By starting at one vowel sound and sliding to another you are making a sliding vowel, or 'diphthong'.

The two sounds, the start point and the end point, effectively give the one sliding vowel two distinct halves, leading to these questions:

- What is the **start** shape and sound?
- What is the **end** shape and sound?
- Is each half of equal **length** and **weight**, or is one half weighted more than the other?
- How does the mouth **move** from A to B?

The sliding vowels are *great* value in accents. You can hear *extraordinary* differences between one region and another. There's just so much room for manoeuvre!

Nothing gives you away in an accent more than getting a sliding vowel wrong. The starting shape may be different from yours, the finishing shape may be different, and the way they get from A to B may be different too. It may even be that where you have a steady vowel they have a slide, or where they slide you're keeping steady!

> *Jan was working with a Welsh actor learning to do a cockney accent. Just when he'd learnt to change his lovely Welsh* sliding *vowel in* MOUTH *to the Cockney* steady *vowel* '**MAAFF**'*, he had to change his* steady *vowel in* FLEECE *to the Cockney* slide '**FLuhEECE**'*! One size does* not *fit all!*

Almost *every word* on the KIT LIST has the potential to be either steady or sliding. But there are some words on the list that are *particularly* good value for money when changing from one accent to another, as the differences can be so extreme. Play with these and you will soon be travelling from Land's End to John o'Groats!

The PRICE vowel

This vowel can reveal *exactly* where you are from, better than a stamp in your passport! As with all sliding vowels, changes in the distance between the start and end shapes and the quality of movement from A to B will change the vowel completely.

> *We (Jan and Edda) both have a slightly rural 'squashed' quality to our* **PRICE** *vowels, and whenever we work together they seem to feed off each other making it more and more obvious where we're from. (Not helpful when you are trying to pass yourself off as a posh voice coach!)*

Listen to these examples saying the phrase: Nice shiny bike.

Hear It [TRACK 63]

    1 Small distance, gentle movement: *Southern Irish* əi

    2 Medium distance, even movement: *Standard American* ai

    3 Large distance, sudden movement: *Cockney* ɑɪ

See It

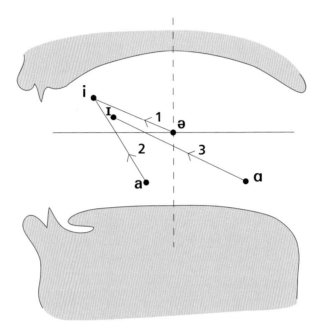

And what about weight distribution? Listen to these examples to hear what we mean:

Hear It [TRACK 64]

    ● Weight all in the first shape: *Yorkshire*

    ● Weight pushing into the second shape: *Berkshire*

And listen carefully, because it may not slide at all:

Hear It [TRACK 65]

    ● *Contemporary London*

HOW TO DO ACCENTS

It's worth knowing that this vowel seems to have a built-in homing device. Maybe it's because we use it in the personal pronoun 'I', connecting it to our sense of self, who knows; but what we do know is that if you don't hang on to that new shape when the emotion kicks in, it will slide back to your own shape quicker than you can blink, and without you even noticing!

The MOUTH vowel

This is another great vowel for playing with start and end shapes. There are so many possibilities!

Feel It

What happens if you make this **sliding vowel** starting from AH and sliding to OO?

- AH-OO: **How now brown cow**
- Now change the starting shape to AA: **Haa-oo Naa-oo Braa-oon Kaa-oo**

Here are some great accent varieties of this one sliding vowel for you to play with:

Hear It [TRACK 66]

Dublin
- E-OO: **Heoow neoow breoon keoow**

Belfast
- AH-EE: **High nigh brine kigh**

And remember…it might not slide at all:

East End London (Cockney)
- AA: **Aa naa braan kaa** (It's a steady vowel!)

All that juice from one little sound. That's the power of the sliding vowel!

The GOAT and FACE vowels

If you travel in a straight line down the *middle* of Britain you will hear these sounds starting life as **steady vowels** in Scotland, gradually opening into small **sliding vowels** south of the border, and becoming larger and larger slides the further south you go.

Hear It [TRACK 67]

Listen to these vowels travel from North to South…

- GOAT
  Scots
  Yorkshire
  Derbyshire
  West Midlands
  London

- FACE
  Scots
  Yorkshire
  Derbyshire
  West Midlands
  London

A similar thing seems to happen in North America too. In the North of Canada these two sounds are steady but by the time you are in Mississippi they are sliding like crazy.

You may even hear one accent start these sliding vowels with the shape another uses to end them. Listen to these diphthongs reverse direction from America to the West Indies:

Hear It [TRACK 68]

- GOAT FACE
  America: Guh-oot Fe-is
  West Indies: Goo-uht Fi-es

What do your **GOAT** and **FACE** do? You can bet they will have to change when you do another accent!

The NEAR–SQUARE–CURE vowels

The first thing you'll notice about these three is they all have an R on the end. That means that these three sounds are only sliding vowels in non-rhotic accents…and even then they may become steady! Confused? Here's a story that will clarify it all. Are you sitting comfortably? Then we'll begin: Once upon a time when all the world was rhotic, these three little sounds all ended in R. But some tongues got weary of regularly rearing and retracting, and so the R was weakened until it finally gave up altogether and all that was left of this once muscular sound was a tiny little schwa. And thus non-rhotics were born. Time marched on, and to this day the story continues. Some tired-out teenage tongues have even wearied of the simple schwa, leaving many young people with just a single steady vowel in place of that once muscular movement.

HOW TO DO ACCENTS

Hear It [TRACK 69]

Listen to us as we go from the R, to the **slide** to the **steady** version of each of these sounds.

- **NEAR**   EE-R   EE-UH   I...
- **SQUARE**   E-R   E-UH   E...
- **CURE**   OO-R   OO-UH   AW

CURE is especially odd because when it becomes steady it's a completely different shape!

The KIT–DRESS–TRAP–BATH vowels

These may not look like sliding vowels to many of you, but if you're from Belfast you may slide your **DRESS**, or if you're a Cockney you may slide your **TRAP**, and they could all slide if you live in the southern states of America. You might even put a Y bounce in-between!

- **TRAP** – trayup

- **DRESS** – dreyus

- **KIT** – kiyut

- **BATH** – bayuth

And last but by no means least...

The GOOSE–FLEECE vowels

Although these never become *huge* slides, they will often slide into position from a schwa, and the contrast between steady versions and sliding versions is very noticeable, as these examples comparing *Welsh* and *Cockney* demonstrate:

Hear It [TRACK 70]

- *Welsh*: blue   goose   neat   fleece
- *Cockney*: blue   goose   neat   fleece

So, for *every* vowel the question is: is it steady or does it slide? And if it slides, learn its:

- **Start and end shapes**

  It is essential to get the right start shape and the right end shape. If the two shapes are close together the slide between them will be more subtle, but if they are far apart your tongue will need to do some shifting! A slide from the centre of the mouth (ə) to EE (i) is a much more subtle movement than a slide from AW (ɔ) to EE (i)!

- **Length and weight**

  The two shapes in a sliding vowel give the sound two halves. Is each half of equal length and weight, or is one given more weight than the other?

- **Quality of movement**

  Is the movement a smooth glide from one shape to the other? Or does it spring like elastic?

A lovely example of steady vowels sliding and vice versa is in the shift from Standard to Southern American, heard in this immortal line from *Forrest Gump*:

> Laaf is laak a bowx of chowclates!

You and the New

Listen to each of the words on the KIT LIST.

- Are some vowels short and some long?

- How do they compare to yours? Longer, Shorter? Steady? Sliding?

- Listen to the speaker in the 'free speech' section. What happens to their vowels when they are stressed? Do they lengthen? Do they stay snappy? Stay steady or start sliding?

HOW TO DO ACCENTS

The Shapes Checklist

Main Shapes Issues

Using a KIT LIST where possible, and whenever you listen to any resource recording, listen for and mimic:

- Vowel shapes and sounds which are different from yours.
- Vowel shapes and sounds which are similar but not quite the same.
- Words that have unexpected vowel shapes and sounds.

For every vowel that is different from yours think about it in these ways:

- **Shape** – Jaw? Tongue? Lips?
- **Length** – Is it longer or shorter than your vowel?
- **Movement** – Are the jaw, tongue and lip shapes fixed, or do they move?
- **Vowel Spectrum** – Where on the spectrum does it belong?

And if it is a sliding vowel learn its:

- **Start and End Shapes**
- **Length and Weight**
- **Quality of Movement**

Main Inventory Issues

- STRUT – FOOT: One vowel or two?
- FOOT – GOOSE – MOUTH: One, two, or three vowels?
- LOT – THOUGHT: One vowel or two?
- PRICE – CHOICE: One vowel or two?
- NURSE-START-NORTH-FORCE-NEAR-SQUARE-CURE (All the words with R!)

    For rhotic accents note the vowel that *precedes* the R (eg **START** takes the **TRAP** vowel in our Southern Irish example). For non-rhotic accents note the vowel that *replaces* the R (eg **NORTH** takes the **THOUGHT** vowel in our Standard English example).

Main Distribution Issues

Which vowel goes with which word in these sets?

- TRAP – BATH – PALM – START
- LOT – CLOTH – THOUGHT – NORTH
- NURSE

  Nurse words: **NURSE BIRD NERVE HEARD FUR WORD**

  Same vowel for each, or different?

The Environmental Issues

- Nasal Colouring
- R Colouring
- The L Effect
- Free or Blocked vowel?
- Stressed or Unstressed syllable?

The Unstressed Word Endings

- Happ**Y**: do they use the **KIT**, **DRESS** or **FLEECE** vowel shape?
- Comm**A**: What is the final shape? Round? Spread?
- Lett**ER**: Is there an R? If not, is it the same as commA?
- Hors**ES**: Is it the **KIT** vowel or a schwa?

You and the New

Inventory

Get to know your own vowel inventory. You only need to do this once and it provides you with a yardstick against which you can compare any new accents. Starting with the word **KIT**, compare the *vowels* in all the words to the *vowel* in the word **KIT** to see, feel and hear if any are the same. Then move onto the word **DRESS** and do the same. Listen and feel for any word that has the same vowel. Once you have done this for the whole list you can add up how many vowels you have.

- How many are short?

- How many are long?

- How many are sliding?

Put this information in the **You and the New** chart at the back of the book.

Using the Spectrum

Can you put your vowels on the spectrum? Which extreme vowel are they closest to? Which are at the front? Which at the back? Which near the middle?

Photocopy the Vowel Spectrum at the back of the book (page 211) and use it to play 'pin the vowel on the map'. (Alternatively, you can download a print-friendly version from www.howtodoaccents.com.) You'll see the places your accent likes to go to and compare them with the places your new accent likes.

6

THE GROOVE

IN THIS CHAPTER...

We will explore the 'music' you play when you create an accent. Every accent has its own music, made from a complex interplay of rhythms and melodies. Think about speech without music: it's robotic, it's just data, empty words. But with music we understand so much more. We know where the thought is heading, what's important and what's not, and not only that, we also know how someone feels about what they are saying. Just like music, each accent has its own distinct style, its own 'language of music'. This is what we call the 'Groove'.

In writing this chapter we are in some ways attempting to define the indefinable. Every accent has a way of using tune and rhythm that is unique, with hundreds of subtle changes, all giving equally subtle changes in meaning. Sometimes neighbouring areas claim to have very different accents from one another, when in fact the differences are really only to be found in the way they groove! However infinite the possibilities, it is possible to break this apparently complex structure down into a simple, step-by-step approach.

Begin by getting the **Big Picture**:

- **Frame it:** Put the cultural, historical and geographical frame around your groove to understand where it comes from.

- **Embody it:** Get a feel for the new groove into your voice and body.

Once you've framed and embodied the *general* features of a groove it is vital to add the detail of **Intonation**:

- **Refine it:** Within the overall features of a groove, refine your ability to listen to and recreate specific intonation patterns.

- **Apply it:** Define the meanings the intonation that patterns convey and apply this to your text.

Don't forget, you've got a groove of your own, of course, which you do without even thinking about it! To do other accents you need to be able to change from your groove to a new one, to play a new 'language of music', and it can sometimes be a little trickier than you think.

A melody that suggests happy confidence in your accent may suggest rude superiority in another. The minor down-and-up slide of Liverpool is considered quite neutral to a Liverpudlian, but in Yorkshire it suggests a somewhat cheeky 'so what, who cares?' attitude.

So when a Liverpudlian actor Edda was working with was playing a boy from Barnsley, his own melodies were great for the scenes where he was being cheeky to his mum, but for the upbeat happy, confident speeches he needed to learn a whole new groove!

The Big Picture

Ever noticed that there is some music you love to dance to and some music that leaves you with two left feet? Picture the scene: you're at a wedding, there's a disco, and the DJ's playing 'something for everyone'. You're having a bit of a giggle at Auntie Mildred and Uncle Stan as they struggle to keep up with the jerky rhythms and frantic pace of the hip-hop grooves, but then on comes a waltz, the tables are turned, and Mildred and Stan look like Fred and Ginger on the dance floor, a sight to behold!

The music we find easy to dance to is familiar: it means something to us. We recognise the beats, we know the moves and we feel safe in the groove of that particular song.

And it can be the same with the groove of an accent: some we will dive into easily; others we may have to learn step by step, just like learning a new dance.

Then imagine the children at the wedding: they seemingly find it effortless to dance to anything. They throw themselves into all the songs, playing and running around, unafraid of what they look like; they simply respond to what they hear and, more importantly, have fun with the new grooves. This is how we suggest you approach your accent grooves, with that same sense of energy and fun.

Frame it

What is it that gives each accent its unique groove? The groove of an accent is born of cultural values, historical legacies and geographical influences, and by framing your accent with these values, legacies and influences you connect the grooves to the people that made them.

The **cultural values** that lie behind an accent may be values such as frugality, self-reliance, hospitality, education or stoicism. These values influence the energy, rhythm and tune of an accent as it moves from moment to moment, from stress point to stress point through the thoughts and words of the speaker.

This is not to say that these are necessarily values that the individual holds, but rather that they are the traditional values of the community that have found expression in the music of the accent. For example, agricultural communities such as Somerset or Saskatchewan need to take a patient long-term approach to life, so often these accents have a slower, more deliberate pace. On the other hand, city communities like New York or London value instant results, making the pace of those accents a lot faster. Yorkshire traditionally prides itself on its down-to-earth, robust approach to life and this finds expression in the accent's weighty, no-nonsense tune and rhythm. Chants and rituals are an important part of Yiddish life, and the accents of Yiddish often retain this 'song-like' use of tune and rhythm. Very different cultures give rise to very different grooves.

The groove's **historical legacies** tell us something of the traders and settlers that have come and gone over time. There is so much to be learned about an accent by looking into the history of the people of the area. Ports are particularly susceptible to these influences. It is noticeable that some of the most striking accents of England are to be found in her busy trading ports. Scandinavian ports have brought their grooves to England, heard in the jumpy rhythms of Newcastle, and the sliding vowels of Liverpool, while the ports of England's West Country have taken their grooves as far afield as Nova Scotia and Barbados.

And don't underestimate the power of **geography** in influencing the way an accent grooves. In the North of Scotland the often harsh living conditions give rise to a need for economy and stoicism which is expressed in clipped, staccato syllables, while the long dark nights give way to community story telling, where dramatic use of tune and rhythm is a real asset! Accents from flat expanses of land such as Norfolk (UK) or Iowa (USA) often use a smaller range of notes with slower pace and extended vowels, whereas areas characterised by hills and valleys such as Wales (UK) and the Ozarks (USA) are noticeably dramatic in their range of notes and use of rhythm.

Finding your groove is about understanding where it comes from, what informs it and what values it expresses. Framing your accent in the cultural, historical and geographical influences that formed it will anchor the roots of the groove and provide a platform from which to take the next steps… **embodying**. Embodying will get those new grooves into your voice and body, and that means getting physical.

Embody it

Different grooves have different energies, dynamics and momentums. In order to explore these successfully we have found that nothing beats getting physical. Speech is a physical act. Taking a physical approach to grooves gets results. The body has an instinct for rhythm and tune that your mind may struggle to interpret. The voice likes to take its lead from the actions of the body. If you want to speak in a new groove, move your body or even just your arm in that groove and the voice will follow.

Actions derived from sports and dance – or other physical movements such as floating, punching, swinging, etc – have often helped us to get the groove into an actor's body, which in turn has helped them to understand and internalise the momentum and music of an accent.

> *When Jan was working with an actor from the RSC whose own Australian accent was leading to a narrow pitch range in his RP, they played with a chiffon scarf, dancing it around like Isodora Duncan, to encourage his range to find the swoops, floats and leaps of pitch used in RP. And when Edda was working with the actor from Liverpool who was playing the kid from Barnsley, they played at shooting with a basketball to encourage his voice to leap up and over in the happy confident speeches, instead of sliding down and up. Although these actors had understood what they ought to be doing with the tune, and were both making fair attempts, it wasn't until they worked physically that they really got impressive results.*

Hear It [TRACK 71] *and Feel It*

Listen to these accents for the energies, dynamics and momentums at work and then have a go at them yourself. We've made suggestions for physical actions.

- *London:* Shadow boxing
- *Liverpool:* Slalom skiing
- *Standard English (RP):* Swinging across monkey bars

These are just our suggestions. The important thing is for you to listen to accents in this way, to get a feel for the groove in your body and find your own physical metaphors to anchor the grooves in your body.

Getting Dynamic

Another great way of getting the groove into your voice and body is to use a simple system of physical dynamics. Fortunately for us a movement expert called Rudolf Laban devised such a system for understanding the way in which a movement is performed! Laban identified three elements with contrasting polar opposites: space, weight and time.

- **Space**: Direct or Indirect
- **Weight**: Heavy or Light
- **Time**: Sudden or Sustained.

These elements combine to form **eight** different physical actions:

 See It

		SPACE	WEIGHT	TIME
	GLIDE	Direct	Light	Sustained
	FLOAT	Indirect	Light	Sustained
	DAB	Direct	Light	Sudden
	FLICK	Indirect	Light	Sudden
	PRESS	Direct	Heavy	Sustained
	WRING	Indirect	Heavy	Sustained
	PUNCH	Direct	Heavy	Sudden
	SLASH	Indirect	Heavy	Sudden

HOW TO DO ACCENTS

These **Effort Actions** are used extensively in drama schools to train actors to change physical manifestations of emotion. We took this idea and applied it to our accent work, using the actions as a shorthand for accessing shifts in the energy, dynamics and momentum of an actor's speech patterns. In one class we asked the students to classify each other's accents according to these actions. There was complete agreement: the Americans were PRESS, the Scots were DABS, the two from Yorkshire were PUNCHES. There was one student from Cork who was a FLICK, and there was even an Italian SLASH!

Hear It [TRACK 72] *and Feel It*

The ability to change the dynamics of your speech is essential if you want to do accents. Do this next exercise in your *own* accent and notice which feel familiar; which feel different, but okay; and which feel downright weird…

- Listen to us speak the days of the week using each of the eight effort actions.
- Practise the physical action as shown in the table above.
- Speak the days of the week while performing the physical action.

Which one feels closest to *your* dynamic? This may be your accent pattern, or it may just be your own personal dynamic. Either way, become aware of it: it is probably a dynamic you use without much thought. To open your potential for doing other accents, learn to enjoy the other dynamic possibilities available to you.

So that's the actions. Here they are again. This time we have connected them to accents so that you can hear how to use them in this context.

Hear It [TRACK 73]

Listen first then have a go at each of the actions yourself. Remember, make the physical actions as you speak; your voice will copy your body!
- *Standard American:* PRESS
- *Scottish:* DAB
- *Contemporary London:* FLICK
- *Yorkshire:* PUNCH
- *Swansea:* SLASH

And how about these?

- *West Midlands:* WRING
- *Essex:* FLOAT
- *Southern Irish:* GLIDE

Exploring the 'Big Picture' groove in this way enables you to make big changes to the pace, rhythm, range and melody with which you speak.

Some grooves may have negative connotations for you. Maybe *you* only 'wring' when you are complaining; maybe *you* only 'punch' when you feel aggressive. Consequently, accents that have these grooves may feel whiney or aggressive to you. It is important to recognise this personal judgement for what it is and then put it to one side. What feels like an aggressive groove to you *doesn't* feel that way to someone whose own groove is always punchy!

Once you have framed the groove and then explored ways of getting it into your body, the next vital step is to add the detail: **Intonation**.

Intonation

In the last section we were exploring the 'Big Picture': getting the feel of the groove into your body and framing it with its cultural and historical roots. This stage is about being more specific.

When you listen to someone speak, you hear **words**, which express literal meaning. You also hear **rhythm** to focus you on specific syllables, and **melody**, which provides more of the attitude and the emotional and sub-textual meaning. The specific combination of rhythm and melody across a phrase of speech is called **Intonation**.

Hear It [TRACK 74]

- **Words**… This is just the words, you can hear the shapes and bite. Some of the accent is there but something's missing…
- **+ Rhythm**… Now I've added the rhythm so now you know which bits to focus on, but it still doesn't sound quite right… I sound a bit like a robot… There's one more thing to add…
- **+ Melody**… And that's the melody. The words and rhythm and melody combined are what make intonation. With all three together you have the whole accent!

HOW TO DO ACCENTS

As J C Wells in his book *English Intonation, An Introduction* (Cambridge University Press, 2006) puts it:

> 'Speakers of English repeatedly face three types of decision as they speak. They are: how to break the material up into chunks, what is to be accented, and what tones are to be used.'

Of course, you make these intonation decisions entirely spontaneously in your own accent, but when you are learning a new accent you may well need to make those decisions in a more conscious way.

Every accent has its own patterns of intonation used to denote different pragmatic meanings. Many accents have very similar patterns, but with some you will notice that the melodies are significantly different from yours. The more unusual the intonation sounds to you, the more attention you need to pay to it.

Intonation is one of the first features of speech we learn as a baby. (Think about the way people talk to babies and dogs!) They are teaching them to recognise meaning not just in the words being said but in the intonation being used. 'It can take children ten years or more to fully grasp all the possible nuances of meaning conveyed by changes in intonation' (David Crystal: *Listen to Your Child*, 1986). You may have only three weeks to grasp those of your new accent, so refining your ability to hear and mimic intonation will clearly be an important skill.

Refining your intonation skills

Listening and mimicking accurately is a vital skill to develop in order to do accents, and it's not as easy as you may think. Can you tell whether the notes in a phrase have gone up or dropped down? Can you recognise which words are being stressed and which are not? And can you identify a chunk? Speech can be divided into chunks. You do not have to listen to whole sentences – after all, some people's sentences ramble on for ever!

We will begin with:

- **What to identify**
  - Identify the chunks.
  - Identify the landing points.
  - Feel the rhythm.

- Play the melody.
- Major or minor?

Then look at:

- **Melody and meaning:**
  - Find neutral.
  - Under or over?
  - What's the attitude? – Playing the action.

What to identify

Identify the chunks

In order to help focus on the use of melody and rhythm you will need to identify the chunks of information within each sentence or phrase. A phrase of speech may be **chunked** in different ways, depending on *how many chunks of information* the speaker decides to present it as. Take the phrase: 'I wear my pants on top of my trousers'. It looks like one phrase, and can be presented as one chunk of information, but a speaker could make it into two, three or more separate chunks of information. Listen to each chunk: it has been selected by the speaker according to the meaning they wish to convey and the response they wish to get. The more new or important information a phrase contains, the more chunks a speaker will make; the more chunks they make, the more words will be emphasised; and the more words that are emphasised, the more emphatic it will sound.

Hear It [TRACKS 75]
- One chunk:

   a) I wear my pants on top of my trousers.
- Two chunks:

   b) I wear my pants | on top of my trousers.
- Three chunks:

   c) I | wear my pants | on top of my trousers.

Can you hear how through the intonation each chunk is presented as a separate, yet still interconnected, piece of information?

HOW TO DO ACCENTS

Feel It

Listen to them again and accurately mimic them.

Identify the landing points

During a chunk the intonation pattern operates a bit like a ball being thrown. *Momentum* is gathered up, the ball is *launched*, it makes a *journey*, it *lands* and *tails* off.

The *principal* focal point in any chunk is the **landing**.

See It

gather			*LAUNCH*		*journey*			***LANDING*** *tail*	
.	.	.	•	.	.	.	.	●	.
I	wear	my	pants	on	top	of	my	**TROU**	sers

(Simple statement of fact)

Change the chunks and you change the meaning. With two landing points you have two chunks of information:

| (first chunk) | | | | | (second chunk) | | | | |

gather		*LANDING* *tail*		–	*gather*			***LANDING*** *tail*	
.	.	•	.	.	.	.	.	●	.
I	wear	MY	pants	on	top	of	my	**TROU**	sers

(Implying: 'Not anyone else's!')

And you may even land on the very first word! Again, two landings make two chunks.

| (first chunk) | | | | (second chunk) | | | | | |

LANDING *and tail...*					*gather* ***LANDING*** *and tail*				
●	.	.	.	.	•	.	.	.	.
I	wear	my	pants	on	**TOP**	of	my	trou	sers

(Implying: 'Where do you wear yours?!')

So, some chunks begin with a **launch**; some gather on the first syllable and head straight to a **landing**. If you feel more than one landing point you have more than one chunk. As you listen to speech in this way you will hear more and more of the possibilities.

Feel the rhythm

Rhythm goes deep into our bodies and operates at a primal level. Get into a person's rhythm and you stand a chance of feeling what they feel – ask Shakespeare! The landing points are, in effect, the stressed syllables in a phrase while the rest of the syllables are unstressed. This interplay of stressed and unstressed syllables creates a basic rhythmic structure through every chunk of speech.

(English is a **stress-timed** language. The stress determines the length of the syllable. **Syllable-timing**, on the other hand, is quite different. Although a syllable may be emphasised using a change in loudness or pitch, the syllable lengths will *not* change. Each syllable is the *same* length *regardless* of emphasis or stress. This means that you give weight to every SYL-LAB-LE, including small words such as **at, from, but, to** and **as**. This can often make the language and accent sound full and dra-ma-tic! Syllable-timed languages include: French, Spanish, Greek, Turkish, Polish, Hindi, Gujarati, Urdu, Punjabi, Bengali, African, Yiddish, Indonesian and Malay.)

Although any speaker may choose the same significant syllables or landing points in a chunk, and therefore the same meaning and basic rhythmic structure, the *feel* of the rhythms in different accents can be very different. Once you have heard where the landing points are and have the basic rhythmic structure of a chunk, you will need to know how to get from one syllable to another. This 'momentum' will be affected by a number of things.

Hear It [TRACK 76]

I wear my pants on top of my trousers.

- **Vowel Lengths:** Short vowels will create a punchy, rapid rhythm (*Cockney*). Vowel extensions on the stressed syllable together with reductions on the unstressed will create a very swingy, on-off rhythmic pattern (*RP*).
- **Consonant Strength:** Strong consonants create weighty movement from syllable to syllable (*Yorkshire*). Loose consonants seem to merge the syllables together (*Liverpool*).

HOW TO DO ACCENTS

- **Glottal Stops:** Glottal stops create a staccato effect; the more there are, the more staccato the rhythm will feel (*Newcastle*).
- **Suspension:** Listen to the way the *Welsh* speaker 'suspends' between the two syllables of Trousers!

It's also worth pointing out at this juncture that not all accents stress *individual words* in the same way. When words have more than one syllable there are choices to make. For example is it **CONtroversy** or **conTROversy**? Is it **CIGarette** or **cigarETTe**? Is it **oFFIcial** or **Official**? Is it **conSERvaTORy** or **conSERvatory**? See what we mean? It may be that the new accent has different rules from yours regarding stress, and these rules can be tricky to identify. Here are a few examples:

- Americans will always use some stress on those **-ory**, **-ony**, **-ary** word endings, where Londoners never would. Word stress can change dramatically from America to the UK, so be careful!

- In Northern English accents you will often hear more syllables in a word being stressed than in Southern English accents. Words with **con-** at the beginning, for example, such as **concern**, **contain**, etc, have one stress in the South of England, but two stresses in the North. This can often give the game away when a Northerner heads South, and vice versa.

- Welsh puts even weight on two syllable words, such as **kitten**, and on the final syllables in a word such as **eleven**, and then also separates those syllables with a small *hiatus* (gap). This creates a lilting, choppy rhythm. You will also hear this pattern in some Scandinavian accents!

And what about 'compound' words? 'What are they?' we hear you cry. This is when two words are brought together to make a third, new word. For example; tooth + brush = **toothbrush**, key + board = **keyboard**. There are also compounds where the words appear separately but still refer to one thing: for example, **egg beater**, **paper bag**, **town hall**, etc. Which half of the compound should you stress? If you are American it's simple: you always stress the first half. But if you are English, on the other hand, more complicated rules will apply. Yes, the English usually stress the first half, but *not* in examples like **paper bag**, or **town hall**. Here's why: if the first word is part of the *fabric* of the second (the bag being *made* of paper), then the second word is stressed; otherwise the first word is. Also, *all* place names in England have the second half stressed, unless the second word is **Street**! Hence it's **OXFORD Street** but it's **Oxford CIRCUS**. Weird, but true!

Needless to say, when you are listening to your resource recording notice if *any* words are stressed in a way that seems unusual to you: there may be a pattern lurking. (And here's where it can be useful to employ an internet search engine to find out more about your accent's stress patterns. You could be surprised: someone somewhere might easily have written a paper or article on the stress patterns of the accent you're working on!)

So, rhythm is created by word stress, sentence stress, vowel length, consonant strength, momentum and flow. Looking back at the Laban work in 'The Big Picture' (pages 153–4) can help you to explore the momentum and flow aspects, looking through 'The Shapes' (page 113) will help with vowel lengths, and try looking at 'The Bite' (page 59) for consonant strength. All of these things come together to create rhythm.

Now we have the words, and we have the rhythm, but we still don't fully have the accent until we have the **Melody**…

Play the melody

It is only when you have the **melody** of a phrase that you will really hear the full accent.

As already explained, the landing point is the most significant syllable in a chunk. The purpose of all our melodies is to lead the listener *to* and *from* this landing point while *also* conveying a whole host of attitudes, emotions and sub-texts. Quite a job! Before you take on the world, start with this simple process. To accurately hear and practise the melodic pattern of a phrase we find it really helps to detach the melody from the words, and then *sing* it. (Yes, we are serious!)

Hear It and See It [TRACK 77]

Listen to us extract the melodic pattern from a *Belfast* and a *London* example:

- Listen to us 'singing' the melody. Notice how we slow right down to check we've got it right…

HOW TO DO ACCENTS

Belfast:

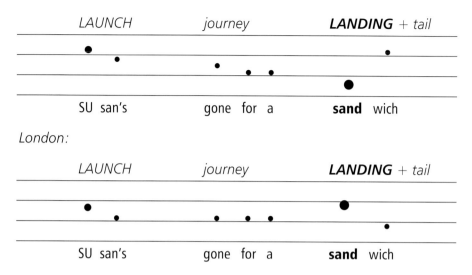

London:

Sing it!

- Have a go yourself at singing the melodic patterns of these two examples (you can do this with any chunk of speech from our sample speakers).

This takes practice and careful listening to pitch movement. When you're out and about, start listening to all the different tunes being used around you and seeing if you can sing them without the words (be discreet though or you might get a mouthful back!). If you have paper to hand, draw a rough musical score: our versions above use four lines (conventional musical staves have five lines, of course), which give plenty of scope to show pitch changes. As you do this you will notice that the rhythm and the melody work hand in hand. For some of you the rhythm may be your anchor, for others the melody, but be sure you are being accurate with both!

Major or minor?

While you are listening to melody you may notice that some tunes have a **Major** quality, while some have a **Minor** quality. Accents operate within different pitch ranges within chunks of speech. Accents operating within small bands within each chunk with small slides between semitone and quarter tones may be described musically as having a **minor** quality (West Midlands, Liverpool), whereas those that have the wider bands with steps between full tones may be described as **major** (London, Edinburgh). Accents that operate within the smaller bands can seem flat, repetitive and even whiney to people who are used to working within larger bands, while large band accents can sound overblown and patronising to those who use a narrow band: in fact they are neither, but this can have the beginnings of a culture clash!

Once you can hear melodies accurately it's time to attach them to meaning. What do those melodies imply?

Melody and meaning

As we have seen, change the landing points and you change the meaning. The same is true of the melody. Even a chunk as small as one word can carry many different meanings.

Hear It [TRACK 78]

> Listen to Edda calling for Jan: you can hear how important melody is for expressing the speaker's attitude and subtext to the listener!

Find neutral

Every accent has a **Neutral** melody: a melody it will use for dispassionate information and simple statements of fact. A 'news-reading' melody, if you like. This is a melody well worth identifying. It will set the 'standard', as it were, against which the other melodies of the accent will contrast.

Under or over?

When listening to the 'neutral pattern' the world of accents divides into two main camps: those that have their landing note **under** the other notes and then *bounce up* on the tail, and those that have their landing note **over** the other notes and then *fall down* on the tail.

HOW TO DO ACCENTS

See It and Hear It [TRACK 79]

UNDER – *Belfast:*

(Accents that follow this pattern are often referred to as having 'upward inflections', because the tail rises up from the low landing point.)

OVER – *London:*

This fundamental difference in the neutral melody (choosing to stress the principal **landing** as either the *lowest* or the *highest* note in the phrase) is vital in distinguishing West Scotland from East Scotland and Northern Ireland from Southern Ireland! The bigger the jump, either up or down, the greater the stress.

TOP TIP

Which of these melodic patterns sounds and feels most like your own?
*Do you use the **under** or **over** pattern when landing in a simple statement?*
Be extra careful: if you are working in an accent that uses the opposite tune pattern from you, it will need more practice!

In any accent if you reverse the final cadence on a simple statement it will turn it into a question without having to change the words! So what sounds like a question in one accent can sound like a statement in the other and vice versa!

Hear It and See It [TRACK 80]

Hear the speakers do it with this simple statement: 'Linda's making the tea', changing it to a question: 'Linda's making the tea?'

Belfast:

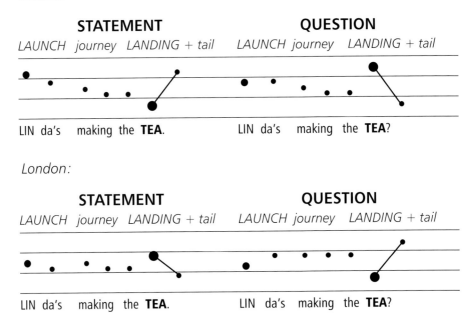

London:

STATEMENT	QUESTION
LAUNCH journey LANDING + tail	LAUNCH journey LANDING + tail

LIN da's making the **TEA**.   LIN da's making the **TEA?**

Feel It

● Have a go at this yourself.

What's the attitude? – Playing the action

One of the biggest mistakes that actors often make is to get stuck in the **Neutral Pattern**. Can you imagine if you spoke in the same melodic pattern for everything you said in your own accent? Or if you just used two melodies – one for a statement, one for a question? It would be robotic and limited, to say the least! And yet we are sure you have heard an actor on stage, from time to time, who has got stuck in the neutral tune of an accent, using it over and over again, no matter what the subtext or emotional journey.

Different melodic patterns are used to let listeners know if the phrase is a statement or a question, and also how the speaker feels and what kind of response may be expected. Although we are calling this the **Attitude**, from

HOW TO DO ACCENTS

the actor's perspective this is the element that expresses the **Action** of a line. Without variation and options all your actions will sound the same!

This aspect of intonation is often what seems to hold actors back, making them feel restricted when working in an accent. There are many degrees of 'knowing' an accent. Being able to truly play with all the possibilities in the melody will give you a real sense of freedom, fun and authenticity.

Some people are lucky enough to hear one or two melodies in an accent and then instinctively know what the other subtle possibilities are, but for many others it will take a little longer, and a lot more listening. There are so many possible subtextual expressions, shock, sarcasm, disappointment, joy, etc, and there are far too many to name. As an actor this is your emotional repertoire. Explore as much of it as you can in order to be fully versed in the emotional language of your accent. Within your own accent this aspect of intonation is second nature; moreover, you are emotionally connected to all your own melodies, they mean something to you.

When working in another groove it is vital to develop your emotional repertoire and make the same emotional connections to the melodies and rhythms of your new accent. Listen to as many chunks as possible on your resource recordings to identify all the variations your speaker uses and why. Below is a list of some of the more basic melodic variations you will need. If you are making your own resource recording try to get the speaker to demonstrate as many of them as possible.

Hear It [TRACK 81]

Overleaf are just some examples of the way intonation can function in Standard English (RP).

Definite Statement (default):

'I like fish and chips'

Interjections: These can have either positive or negative implications.

'Right…' 'Really…' 'Yes…'

Exclamations:

'I don't believe it!'

Tentative Statement: Implies you're not sure or there's something you're not saying! For instance, answering the question 'Is he attractive?' with:

'Well, he wears nice clothes.'

The tune would imply that he may not be that attractive!

Yes/No Interrogative Questions: Questions that require a 'yes' or 'no' answer.

Q: 'Do you like peas?'

Wh' Questions: Requiring more information than just 'yes' or 'no'.

Q: 'What time is it?'
Q: 'Where are you?'
Q: 'When did you arrive?'
Q: 'Who's there?'
Q: 'Why are you laughing?'
Q: 'How old are you?'

Implicational Tone: Implies there's more to come (and often leads to a small encourager from the listener!). This is used for lists until the final item when the tune returns to the statement!

'He knocked on the door…(yes)… turned the handle…stepped into the house…'

Declarative Question: It *looks* like a statement but the *tune* makes it a question!

'We're leaving now?'

Tags: Short additions added to the end of a phrase to either:

A Ask for confirmation: 'We've been here before, haven't we?'
B Declare expected agreement: 'We've been here before, haven't we.'

Command:

'Put that down!'

All that communication, and it's the intonation that does it! This is by no means a definitive list, but it can give you a good basic intonation vocabulary.

When you are listening to your resource recording, identify and listen to individual chunks of speech one at a time so that you can really pay attention to them. Any recording will have chunks of many different lengths, with all kinds of meanings, each one giving you insights into the specific grooves used in that accent.

Remember:

> 'Speakers of English repeatedly face three types of decisions as they speak. They are: how to break the material up into chunks, what is to be accented, and what tones are to be used.'

In our own accents we make all these decisions entirely unconsciously, and as such we have deep emotional and psychological connections to our own use of rhythm and melody. Therefore it is important to build emotional and psychological connections with the uses of rhythm and melody in any new accent you work in.

The Groove Checklist

- What is/are the **Laban** effort action/s for the accent?
- Does the accent stress **under** or **over** the phrase in basic statements of fact?
- Does the accent use **major** or **minor** inflections in basic statements?
- Is the pace fast or slow, evenly paced or varied?
- Is the pitch range large or small?

You and the New

As you make discoveries about the groove of your new accent, don't forget to compare it to your own. Remember that the same physical pattern of rises and falls, stressed and unstressed syllables, may have one meaning in your accent but quite a different meaning in the new one. Knowing how your intonation patterns compare to those of your new accent will help you focus on those areas where your two accents differ most.

Most accent books and CDs will give little if any information on the complex intonation patterns possible in an accent. At best they may describe the neutral pattern. For you to do any accent well you need to develop your ear for rhythm and melody and how to connect this to thoughts in different patterns from your own.

7

GET PROFESSIONAL

IN THIS CHAPTER...

Assuming you aren't simply doing accents as a hobby, you will also need to know how to take your work in the professional arena to a professional level. This means knowing not just how to **do** an accent, but also how to **work on** it to keep improving it and how to **work with** it in different professional contexts.

First of all we will give you advice on how to practise: after all, if you want to be professional at something you have to practise.

We then take you through what to do when your accent meets the specific demands of:

- the production
- the director
- the rehearsal
- the character.

And finally:

- How to handle an audition.
- How to handle sight-reading.

Get Practising

It ought to go without saying (but it often doesn't) that if you want to be good at something it takes practice. This doesn't mean having to sit for hours labouring over your script: it simply means building a little bit of accent practice into your daily routine.

It is absolutely essential to practise both on and off your text. If the only things you can say in the accent are the words in your script, you do not know the accent and your performance will be limited. What happens when someone forgets their cue and you have to ad lib? Or there's a re-write, or a cut reappears? You're scuppered!

So, here's our advice for accent practice.

Any time, anywhere

- Have a 'springboard sentence' in the accent. This is a short phrase that automatically gets the accent into your mouth, seemingly without you being involved. Your brain associates that phrase with the accent and as soon as you say it that 'accent file' in your head downloads and opens up. This is invaluable for those moments when you seem to go adrift and need to 'reboot' the accent.

At home

- Listen to your accent resource a little every day. You can do this while you're getting a meal ready, in the car, at the gym, even as you go to sleep; anywhere that makes it easy and regular. It is vital to give your brain something to refer to and feed off (see 'Making and using a resource recording' in 'Getting Started', page 26).

- Narrate your day: 'I think I'll just put the kettle on', 'Oh, that's the phone, I'll just answer it', and so on. Notice and correct any mistakes as you make them. It's crucial not to reinforce bad habits but to teach yourself the new patterns. Horsey types will tell you that if you let a horse refuse a jump once the chances are it will refuse it again, and we can tell you that your mouth behaves in much the same way. Remember just like the rider, you are the one in charge, not your mouth, so make sure you *always* correct it at every jump!

- If there's a group of you learning the accent, have an accent evening: you could cook the food, listen to the music, watch the movies, whatever takes your fancy. Any excuse for a party!

- Don't just practise the bits you're good at. Focus on different elements of the accent – the Foundations, the Major Players, vowel Shapes or the Groove.

Out in the real world

- Read billboards, adverts, notices and other short bursts of text either out loud or in your head. This trains you to translate from the written word into the new spoken patterns of an accent.

- Look out for specific sounds and see if you can identify them on billboards, etc.

- Ask for directions, or for assistance in a shop.

With the Set Text

- Practise with the Set Text found in the Appendix (page 208). This contains all the sounds and combinations of the sounds in English, so once you can say this you can you say everything!

- Record yourself. Play it back and be your own judge. If you don't convince yourself you won't convince anyone else either!

- If you used the Set Text to make your own resource recording, play it frequently while you read and speak along with it. You will learn so much in terms of the specific articulation of vowels, consonants and combinations, and also in the overall use of energy, tune, etc.

- The more you work with the Set Text, the more you will get to know it. Once you can confidently recite it in the accent it will be invaluable as warm-up and practice material.

On the script

Eventually, of course, your words will be connected to emotional impulses, but there is also a certain amount of basic technical gymnastics that your mouth is going to have to get used to before you get there. This may be more or less challenging depending on the accent you are doing and your familiarity with it. Sometimes you need to let yourself off the 'emotional' hook and work on your script technically. This is only the same as doing table work and blocking in rehearsals. You do it with the acting, so do it with the accent.

- To begin with you may want to read very slowly out loud in your new accent, a little like a child learning to read, plotting your way through the sounds.

- Work on your text phrase by phrase (see 'The Groove' for 'Identify the chunks', page 158, and 'Intonation', page 156).

- Identify the words in the phrase that take the stress. These will be the most noticeable and also the simplest. They will also be the anchor sounds in the phrase. (These stresses are only temporary, as things may change during rehearsals, but you need them as a starting point.) Practise these words first so that you are confident in making the shapes and sounds. They will provide solid stepping stones through the text.

The gymnastics routine

Practising your text is very much like practising a gymnastics tumbling routine. To begin with, you have to practise each of the moves separately before you can string them together. Once you are confident you stand at one corner of the floor mat, looking at the 'phrase' to be performed between there and the far corner. You breathe and… GO!…, landing with aplomb at the far corner. If anything does go wrong you know that bit needs reworking until the whole sequence is flawless. This is the process:

- Identify the 'big moves' in the routine, the triple sukahara, the double back flip and the handspring! These may be words you find tricky, or specific vowels or consonant combinations.

- Work on each of these moves separately until your mouth can do them smoothly.

- Practise getting both to and from each of these moves until you can get through the whole phrase fluently. If you falter, stumble or trip, keep going back to step two until you can say the whole phrase without tripping.

- Once you are confident with the technical aspect of the gymnastics the next step for a perfect 10 is to do it 'once more with feeling'. If when you connect to the emotional drive of the line things begin to slip, go back and look at those bits again. Connect the sound firmly to the feeling so that the two things becomes one.

Accent meets production

Over the years we have probably worked with many different kinds of actor and director, each with their own working process. Whatever that process may be, during any rehearsal period it is the actor's job to layer the journey of their character into the world of the play and the particular demands of the production.

Working with an accent adds another layer that will need to be woven into this process. It can be quite a delicate juggling act and one that will need careful consideration. On the one hand you don't want the accent to get in the way of your ability to focus, but on the other hand you want to be sure the accent is an integral part of the character. And of course, by the time you are in front of an audience you want the accent to be bedded in and authentic.

There is a lot to consider, and each of us finds our own way through, so here are some handy hints for getting the most out of yourself and your accent.

Accent meets director

You may work with some very different directorial approaches. We have known directors who:

- **Want you to speak all the time in the accent when in the rehearsal room.**

  This can be heaven or hell. Experience tells us that at its worst this approach will ingrain bad habits which become fixed and difficult to correct. At best, however, it can be an opportunity to make an accent feel as natural as your own speech. If this is what your director wants, you will need to be *very* disciplined. Whenever you are using the accent you are effectively working on it. It is tough to have to concentrate this hard on the accent all day, every day. It may be a good idea to record the rehearsal so that you can listen to it later and notice where you are making mistakes. It can also help to have an 'accent buddy' in the cast who you can ask to give you feedback on particular sounds or scenes that you are struggling with. Whatever you do, don't think that because you are using the accent all the time you don't need also to work on the specifics in a structured, focused way: you do!

- **Don't want you to use the accent for the first week.**

    This is a very popular approach with directors. Be sure that you use your home time well to work on the accent and the text, as once they do ask you to use it they will expect the accent to be great! (See 'Get Practising', page 173.)

- **Wish they didn't have to deal with the accent at all!**

    This is the director that doesn't want to know about the accent, has had bad experiences with dialect coaches, or has seen good actors go bad simply because of the accent! Well, that's a tricky one: you will have to work independently and not expect any support. Try not to be dispirited by this and don't take it personally.

- **Want to give you accent notes.**

    Be grateful for the interest but know that they may not be the most sensitive or helpful remarks! If you are lucky enough to have a coach working on the show make sure you explain what your director has asked for so that together you can solve whatever problems arise.

Every director is unique, as is every actor, so whatever is happening make sure you are taking responsibility for yourself and your accent work. Look at 'Get Practising' (page 173) to find suggestions for structured ways of working. The one thing we can say for certain is that you *cannot* start work on the accent too soon!

Accent meets rehearsal

Always warm up your accent before rehearsals begin. It can take a good ten minutes of talking in an accent before you are fully engaged with it.

Of course, in rehearsal you are two people, yourself and the character ('You and the New'):

- When you are yourself, talking as yourself, it helps to have a 'springboard sentence' to get back into the accent when the scene starts again (see 'Any time, anywhere', page 173).

- When you are in character, but not actually speaking, maybe you are pausing, thinking, relaxing, or listening in a scene, **don't relax out of the muscular setting** of the accent! Remember, the setting of the accent *is* the relaxed setting of your character's face. Likewise, if you 'uhm' and 'erm' the sound you hear should be the hesitation sound of the accent, not your own.

If you have time between scenes when you are not called, you can use it to listen to your resource recording and practise your accent on or off script. If your accent is getting in the way of your work in a scene it is a clear sign that you need to do more work outside rehearsals. During the rehearsal of a scene is *not* the time to do this kind of work.

Accent meets character

Age, gender, class, profession, family background and personal aspirations will all make a difference to the way someone sounds. Whatever acting process you have, connect your accent study to your character study.

Some actors use the following exercise to develop a character history/profile and it can also be a great way of getting to know the manner in which your character communicates.

- What do I say about other people?
- What do others say about me?

When you have answered those questions by looking through your script, find qualities within the accent that will help you portray them. Knowing the variety of 'T' formations in a London accent, for example, combined with little shifts in tune, can be great for conveying various emotional subtexts: 'It doesn't ma**?**er' (neutral); 'It doesn't ma**dd**er' (ingratiating); 'It doesn't ma**tt**er' (aggressive)! The same person can and will use all three varieties, depending on how they feel. If your character is given to being more aggressive or pushy, you will know which one to use!

On the other hand, you may think of the accent you are using as 'friendly', 'warm' and 'cuddly' but your character is referred to by others as 'spiteful', 'short-tempered' and 'cold'. Try to figure out what qualities within the accent can help you to portray these qualities. It may be in the groove or the consonant quality or simply the pace of delivery.

> *Jan was working on the RSC production of* Merry Wives the Musical. *One of the characters is called Pistol, so named because of his swaggering quick-fire repartee. The director wanted the actor playing Pistol to do a cockney accent. Using the punchy rhythms within the accent helped the actor find the much-needed personality traits of his character. Remember, the accent can serve the character. If you get to know the accent inside out you will see what it has to offer and how best to utilise it!*

If you can find a buddy, 'hot-seat' each other in the accent. This helps you to develop spontaneity and inner connection.

Accent meets audition

You may have two weeks to prepare for an audition or you may have two days. You may be asked for a speech, or you may be asked to sight-read.

Ask yourself this question: **'How good am I at this accent?'** (be honest with yourself). Only then you can assess how much work you have to do and how much time you have to do it in.

There is always time to do something useful, even if you only have a day:

- Find a recording of the accent somewhere (see 'Working with a resource recording' (page 25) for ideas).
- Check though the 'Major Players', especially the L (page 71) and the R (page 61).
- Get a sense of the 'Big Picture' groove (page 151).
- Decide on a couple of key vowel sounds.
- Find a 'springboard sentence' (page 173) to get you into the accent.

These form the basis of an accent. The more time you have, the more detail you can go into.

On the day

Before you go into the casting/audition make sure you have warmed the accent up, that you've got your springboard sentence and that the accent is ready to be switched on. It is a tall order to expect to be able to pull it out of the bag the moment you open your mouth.

If it is a sight-reading audition (aagghhh!), the assumption is that you can do the accent. You must have said you can or you wouldn't be there in the first place. The chances are they will give you the text to look at just before you go in. Make sure you get what you do know of the accent into your system: read the script out loud; get it into your mouth and body; feel the muscularity, the zone and the energy and direction of flow. But remember: the purpose of sight-reading is to demonstrate your talents as an actor and your suitability for the role. Focus on your acting and script skills. The odd mistakes in an accent will be forgiven if you have shown willing and are acting with integrity.

Don't forget to act!

Even a polished accent can have its downside. Actors can get carried away by the sound of the accent and forget some of the most basic acting prerequisites such as: listen and respond; be in the moment; connect to the impulse; remember what you want; etc.

Here are some basic script-skills that will at least keep you connected to the drive of the text:

- Notice sentence lengths, punctuation, odd word use, etc.
- Mark the important/significant words.
- Mark the word at the end of each phrase and head towards it. The last word is so much more important than the first in terms of connection.
- Mark crescendos and changes of gear. Know the journey that your feelings and thoughts will move in.

While reading:

- Slow down your breathing. The most common mistake is to go too fast!

HOW TO DO ACCENTS

- Don't worry *at all* about being perfect. Be as good as you are. No better, no worse.

Finally, remember, they are interested in you as an *actor*, and will be more interested in an intelligent, professional approach to the accent and the acting. Having someone with potential is more important than having someone polished.

APPENDIX

What happens next?

Congratulations! You have navigated your way around all the structures and processes of accents! Phew! You have developed new muscular awareness, you have expanded your flexibility and above all you have learned the architecture of accents.

At the very beginning of this book we said, 'Acting with an accent can be a dream or a nightmare for an actor', and in some ways this book may have had moments of both for you. Along with all the 'Well I never!', 'Who'd a thunk it?' moments you may well have had some nightmarish, 'What the @@**?', 'I just don't get it!' moments too. Don't despair. Contained within this book are *all* the tools you need to create honest, authentic connected accents. Some of the tools will act like instant coffee, while others may need percolating a little longer. Keep dipping in, revisiting, exploring, and bit by bit, through a combination of understanding the processes and putting them into practice, you can teach both your brain and your body how to do accents.

The advantages are huge. No more flailing around in the dark hoping you know what you're doing. No more going to dialect coaches wishing you knew more so that you can understand what they are saying! You now have a structure that you can apply to any accent.

The points of change from one accent to another may be many or few, but they can all be found within this basic architecture:

- Foundations
- Two Planets
- The Bite
- The Shapes
- The Groove.

What follows next are all the extras:

- You and the New chart (pages 187–95).
- Example chart filled in with two contrasting accents (pages 196–205).
- Everything you need to make a resource recording: the KIT LIST, the questions to get your speakers talking, the Major Player elicitation sentences and the Set Text (pages 206–8).

- Selected internet accent resources (page 209).

- Handy maps of rhotic and non-rhotic areas of the UK and America (page 210).

- A full size vowel spectrum for charting your own and any new vowels you hear (page 211).

- Space Exploration pages for fuller exploration of your vowel space (pages 212–20).

HOW TO DO ACCENTS

You and the New chart

	ACCENT
YOU	
NEW	

The Foundations

	ZONE	TONE	SETTING	DIRECTION
YOU				
NEW				

The Bite

The Two Planets + Which R R U?

	RHOTIC	NON-RHOTIC		WHICH R? – WHICH ZONE?
		+Linking bounce	+Intrusive bounce	
YOU				
NEW				

The Major Players

Patterns	L				NG				TH						H
	1 Only Light L 2 Only Dark L 3 Light and Dark L 4 Light L and W Sub				1 Hard in NG and ING words 2 Soft in NG and ING words 3 Hard In NG words and dropped in ING words 4 Soft in NG words and dropped in ING words				1 Standard TH's everywhere 2 Plosive TH's everywhere 3 T/D Substitutes – Change to *T and D* everywhere 4 Voiced TH – Changes to *D* at the start of a word, but *V* in the middle and end. Voiceless TH: Changes to *F* everywhere. 5 Voiced TH – **dropped** at the start of a word and *V* in the middle and end. Voiceless TH – changes to *F* everywhere						
	1	2	3	4	1	2	3	4	1	2	3	4	5	Other	Drop or not?
YOU															
NEW															

The Glottal Stop

	replace a T	accompany a T, P or K	replace any other sound or word
YOU			
NEW			

HOW TO DO ACCENTS

YOOs

	YOOs everywhere	Dropped after L and S	Dropped after L and S Crunched after T and D	Dropped after *all* gum-ridge consonants: S Z N T D L and THs
YOU				
NEW				

The Shapes

Kit List

	YOU	NEW
KIT		
DRESS		
STRUT		
FOOT		

	YOU	NEW
GOOSE		
FLEECE		
NURSE		
TRAP		
BATH		
PALM		

HOW TO DO ACCENTS

Kit List (continued)

	YOU	NEW
START		
LOT		
CLOTH		
THOUGHT		
NORTH		
FORCE		

Kit List (continued)

	YOU	NEW
FACE		
GOAT		
PRICE		
CHOICE		
MOUTH		
NEAR		

HOW TO DO ACCENTS

Kit List (continued)

	YOU	NEW
SQUARE		
CURE		

The Shapes

Main Inventory Issues

	STRUT – FOOT One vowel or two?	**FOOT – GOOSE – MOUTH** One, two, or three vowels?	**LOT – THOUGHT** One vowel or two?	**PRICE – CHOICE** One vowel or two?
YOU				
NEW				

Main Distribution Issues

Which vowel shape goes with which word in these sets?

	TRAP	**BATH**	**PALM**	**START**
YOU				
NEW				

	LOT	**CLOTH**	**THOUGHT**	**NORTH**
YOU				
NEW				

'R' WORDS

For RHOTIC accents note the vowel that precedes the R (eg START takes TRAP vowel in our Southern Irish example). For non-rhotic accents note the vowel that replaces the R (eg NORTH takes the THOUGHT vowel in our Standard English example).

	NURSE	START	NORTH	FORCE
YOU				
NEW				

	NEAR	SQUARE	CURE
YOU			
NEW			

The UNSTRESSED Word Endings

	happY KIT, DRESS or FLEECE vowel?	commA What is the final shape?	lettER Is there an R? If not, is it the same as commA?	horsES Is it the KIT vowel or a SCHWA?
YOU				
NEW				

HOW TO DO ACCENTS

The Groove

	LABAN ACTION	MAJOR OR MINOR?	UNDER OR OVER?
YOU			
NEW			

Specific Intonation Notes

Any other notes and observations…

Writing down vowel sounds

How can you write down vowel sounds? If we write AW and ask you all to read it out loud there will be many different sounds being made. So how do you write the difference between the vowel in **HOT** and the vowel in **THOUGHT** (if there is one)?

The important thing when writing sounds for yourself is to use symbols and letters that mean something to you.

Some of you may be familiar with the use of phonetic symbols to describe speech sounds. These provide an excellent neutral way of being precise about which sound is being used so that anyone who reads it knows which sound is being referred to. The International Phonetic Association divides and labels the vowel space like this:

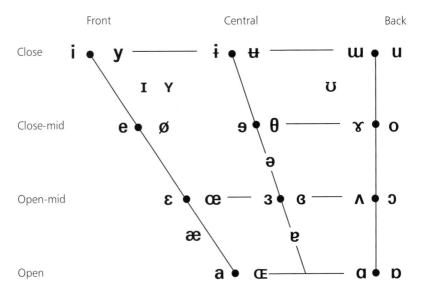

Where symbols appear in pairs, the one on the right represents a rounded vowel.

The words on the left (open, open-mid, close-mid, close) indicate the position of the jaw and height of the tongue. The words across the top (front, central, back) indicate the position of the hump in the tongue.

You will recognise the symbols around the outside of this chart as the extreme vowels we explored in The Shapes (page 131).

We will use the symbols from this chart to describe vowel sounds on the KIT LIST example breakdown. We will also use longhand to describe what we hear.

HOW TO DO ACCENTS

You and the New Charts – Sample

	ACCENT
YOU	London (East London)
NEW	Standard American

The Foundations

	ZONE	TONE	SETTING	DIRECTION
YOU	3	Brass Band	Jaw feels held Lips are flat and thin Soft Palate low 'aaw'	Punched up onto the hard palate and then drives forward onto the teeth but stays there bit like getting trapped behind the tube doors!
NEW	4	Full, slight twang, bit of a honk bit like a duck	Jaw close together Lips are flat Energy in the cheeks Soft palate low	Think of surround speakers in the back of the head to get full oral and back of nose resonance then drive the sound forward and wide in the mouth

The Bite

The Two Planets + Which R R U?

	RHOTIC	NON-RHOTIC		WHICH R? – WHICH ZONE?
		+Linking bounce	+Intrusive bounce	
YOU	No	yes	yes	Always substitute – zone 1
NEW	Yes	No	NO	Always molar – zone 3

Major Players

Patterns	L	NG	TH	H
	1 Only Light L 2 Only Dark L 3 Light and Dark L 4 Light L and W Sub	1 Hard in NG and ING words 2 Soft in NG and ING words 3 Hard In NG words and dropped in ING words 4 Soft in NG words and dropped in ING words	1 Standard TH's everywhere 2 Plosive Th's everywhere 3 T/D Substitutes – Change to *T and D* everywhere 4 Voiced TH – Changes to *D* at the start of a word, but *V* in the middle and end. Voiceless TH: Changes to *F* everywhere. 5 Voiced TH – *dropped* at the start of a word and *V* in the middle and end. Voiceless TH – changes to *F* everywhere	

	1	2	3	4	1	2	3	4	1	2	3	4	5	Other	Drop or not?
YOU	4				4				5						yes
NEW	3				2				1						no

The Glottal Stop

	replace a T	accompany a T, P or K	replace an F or TH
YOU	always	Yes a lot of the time	'To' With a glottal
NEW	No	No	No

HOW TO DO ACCENTS

YOOs

	YOOS everywhere	Dropped after L and S	Dropped after L and S Crunched after T and D	Dropped after **all** gum-ridge consonants: S Z N T D L and THs
YOU			Drop and crunch	
NEW				Drop

The Shapes

Kit List

	YOU	NEW
KIT	I It feels <u>short</u> and punchy quite close to i on the spectrum	I <u>Short</u>, it feels more relaxed, very slight 'uh' on the end.
DRESS	ɛ <u>Short.</u> It feels near to the 'e' on the spectrum.	ɛ <u>Short</u>, though a little longer than mine. And feels a little closer to '**a**'.
STRUT	ʌ <u>Short</u> UH – quite open, slight A sound to it.	ʌ <u>Short</u> UH – basically the same...maybe a little less open
FOOT	ʊ <u>Short.</u> Lip pouts a tiny bit.	ʊ <u>Short</u>, not very different from mine.

Kit List (continued)

	YOU	NEW
GOOSE	əu Sliding. Long I've got a tiny schwa before the /oo/ vowel. My lips start relaxed and then round a tiny bit.	uː Steady. Long. Soft round lips. Sound feels further back.
FLEECE	əi Sliding. I start from UH in the centre and then slide to EE	iː Steady and long. Feels it very close to I on the spectrum.
NURSE	3ː Long, steady. Feel my lips pout a bit.	3˞ Long and steady but it just feels like a molar R on its own!
TRAP	æ Short, close to my DRESS sound.	æ Short. Doesn't feel any different!
BATH	aː Long, steady. My lips round a bit, jaw open. Feel It at the back.	æ Seems the same as the TRAP vowel to me.
PALM	aː Same as BATH	aː Long and steady. Same as mine!

HOW TO DO ACCENTS

Kit List (continued)

	YOU	NEW
START	aː Same as BATH and PALM	ɑr Vowel feels the same as PALM but I need to add the R, and start it while I'm doing the vowel.
LOT	ɒ _Short._ My jaw is open, I feel my cheeks come in a bit and my lips round a bit.	a _Short and steady._ Like my BATH vowel.
CLOTH	ɒ _Same as LOT_	a Feels the same as LOT.
THOUGHT	ɔu _Sliding_ Cheeks pull in, lips round and then tighten.	ɑ Seems the same as LOT and CLOTH.
NORTH	As above	ɔr Same as my THOUGHT vowel but with an added molar r
FORCE	As above	As above

Kit List (continued)

	YOU	NEW
FACE	**æi** Sliding. It feels close to **a** on the spectrum and ends in i . I hit the first half and jump quickly to the second half.	**εi** sliding. It starts closer to 'e' on the spectrum and ends in 'i'- ee. It feels equal on both halves and moves smoothly.
GOAT	**ʌʊ** Sliding I drop my jaw open and then close it with a little bit of lip-rounding.	**ou** Sliding Feels like one sound. Starts round and then rounds even more.
PRICE	**ɑɪ** Sliding. Starts where my BATH vowel is and then my tongue bounces to my KIT vowel. Lips tighten across teeth.	**ai** Sliding, Starts nearer the TRAP vowel and glides smoothly to their FLEECE vowel. Equal glide.
CHOICE	**ɔi** sliding Starts at my THOUGHT and ends at FLEECE. Jumps from one to the other.	**ɔi** sliding same shapes but a smooth glide from one to the other.
MOUTH	**æː** Long and Steady Just like my TRAP vowel but long.	**aʊ** Sliding A smooth glide from TRAP vowel to FOOT vowel.
NEAR	**ɪː** Long and steady version of my KIT vowel. (Unless I'm cross then it's 'eeyuh'!)	**ir** It feels like it starts with the KIT vowel then I have to add molar r.

HOW TO DO ACCENTS

Kit List (continued)

	YOU	NEW
SQUARE	**eː** Long version of my DRESS vowel, with a very slight slide to UH at the end	**er** It's their DRESS vowel with a molar r added
CURE	**ɔː** Like my THOUGHT vowel.	OO then an a followed by an r

The Shapes

Main Inventory Issues

	STRUT – FOOT One vowel or two?	FOOT – GOOSE – MOUTH One, two, or three vowels?	LOT – THOUGHT One vowel or two?	PRICE – CHOICE One vowel or two?
YOU	2	3	2	2
NEW	2	3	1	2

Main Distribution Issues

Which vowel shape goes with which word in these sets?

	TRAP	BATH	PALM	START
YOU	Short A	Long AH	Long AH like BATH	Long AH like BATH
NEW	Shortish A, longer than mine tho'	Shortish A like TRAP	Long AH bit rounder than mine.	Long AH Like PALM but with R

	LOT	CLOTH	THOUGHT	NORTH
YOU	Round short, jaw open	Exactly the same as LOT	Longish, lips very rounded	Exactly like THOUGHT
NEW	Open AH, like my BATH	Open AH	Open AH	Like mine but with R

'R' Words

For RHOTIC accents note the vowel that precedes the R (eg START takes TRAP vowel in our Southern Irish example). For non-rhotic accents note the vowel that replaces the R (eg NORTH takes the THOUGHT vowel in our Standard English example).

	NURSE	START	NORTH	FORCE
YOU	no	no	no	no
NEW	Yes – it's only an R with no vowel shape	Yes – feels a bit like a LOT vowel.	Yes – my vowel followed by R	Yes – my vowel followed by R

	NEAR	SQUARE	CURE
YOU	no	no	no
NEW	Yes – KIT vowel followed by R	Yes – DRESS vowel followed by R	Yes – my THOUGHT vowel followed by R

The UNSTRESSED Word Endings

	happY KIT, DRESS or FLEECE vowel?	commA What is the final shape?	lettER Is there an R? If not, is it the same as commA?	horsES Is it the KIT vowel or a SCHWA?
YOU	fleece	opens towards A	Same as comma	kit
NEW	fleece	a little less open and feels further back	Molar r	schwa

The Groove

	LABAN ACTION	MAJOR OR MINOR?	UNDER OR OVER?
YOU	punchy	major	over
NEW	Press	major	over

Specific Intonation Notes

Any other notes and observations...

American drives through to the end of the line. More words are stressed. It's a lot more direct. More stress on the personal pronoun.

Make your own Resource Recording

The KIT LIST

1	KIT	13	CLOTH
2	DRESS	14	THOUGHT
3	STRUT	15	NORTH
4	FOOT	16	FORCE
5	GOOSE	17	FACE
6	FLEECE	18	GOAT
7	NURSE	19	PRICE
8	TRAP	20	CHOICE
9	BATH	21	MOUTH
10	PALM	22	NEAR
11	START	23	SQUARE
12	LOT	24	CURE

(NB: In his book *Accents of English: An Introduction* (Cambridge University Press, 1982), the originator of the KIT LIST, J C Wells, includes a series of **KIT LIST sets** – a long list of words, subdivided into groups, whose vowels in Standard English and Standard American share the same sounds as the vowels in the 24 words above. An adapted and expanded version of Professor Wells' sets can be found on the *How to Do Accents* website, at www.howtodoaccents.com/kitlistsets.)

Questions to get your speakers talking

- What food do you most miss from home?
- What sort of scenery and landscape do you have in your area?
- What's your ideal home?
- What music do you like/dislike?
- What qualities do you value in a friendship?
- What 'bad habits' do you dislike in a person?
- How do you think your accent is perceived by others?
- What was your favourite childhood game/toy?

Major Player elicitation sentences

- **R:** Margaret, Linda and Gerry asked Peter if Roland started with 'R'.
- **L:** Larry the silly lamb slept peacefully in the field until hailstones fell.
- **H:** Harry Hobson had a holiday in Hawaii.
- **NG:** The singer was singing for the king.
- **TH:** That's my brother with a thermos of Matthew's broth.

Set Text: Arthur the Rat

There was once a young rat named Arthur, who could never take the trouble to make up his mind. Whenever his friends asked him if he would like to go out with them, he would only answer, 'I don't know.' He wouldn't say 'yes' and he wouldn't say 'no' either. He could never learn to make a choice.

His aunt Helen said to him, 'No one will ever care for you if you carry on like this. You have no more mind than a blade of grass.' Arthur looked wise, but said nothing.

One rainy day, the rats heard a great noise in the loft where they lived. The pine rafters were all rotten, and at last one of the joists had given way and fallen to the ground. The walls shook and all the rats' hair stood on end with fear and horror. 'This won't do,' said the old rat who was chief, 'I'll send out scouts to search for a new home.'

Three hours later the seven scouts came back and said, 'We have found a stone house, which is just what we wanted; there is room and good food for us all. There is a kindly horse named Nelly, a cow, a calf, and a garden with an elm tree.' Just then the old rat caught sight of young Arthur. 'Are you coming with us?' he asked. 'I don't know.' Arthur sighed. 'The roof may not come down just yet.' 'Well,' said the old rat angrily, 'we can't wait all day for you to make up your mind; right about face! March!' And they went off.

Arthur stood and watched the other rats hurry away. The idea of an immediate decision was too much for him. 'I'll go back to my hole for a bit,' he said to himself, 'just to make up my mind.'

That night there was a great crash that shook the earth and down came the whole roof. Next day some men rode up and looked at the ruins. One of them moved a board and under it they saw a young rat lying on his side, quite dead, half in and half out of his hole.

HOW TO DO ACCENTS

Selected internet accent resources

- **http://accent.gmu.edu**
  The Speech Accent Archive is a project of the Center for History and New Media. It presents a large set of speech samples from a variety of language backgrounds. Native and non-native speakers of English read the same paragraph and are carefully transcribed.

- **www.bbc.co.uk**
  This is a good website generally. You can listen to interviews on Radio 4 and check out the excellent 'Routes Of English' series that has some great samples and background information on accents and dialects of English. (You can in fact buy this series in book and CD form.)

- **www.bbc.co.uk/voices**
  The clips are drawn from the 'Voices' recordings – which capture 1,200 people in conversation. There's a great map that you can 'hover' over to locate the samples you're looking for.

- **www.bl.uk/learning/langlit/ sounds**
  www.collectbritain.co.uk/ collections/dialects
  These are the British Library websites with some lovely archive recordings of British accents and dialects.

- **www.google.com / www. google.co.uk**
  Put in the name of the accent you are looking for together with the words 'accent' or 'dialect' and see what you get!

- **www.youtube.com**
  You will find people demonstrating their accents all over the place on this site, either deliberately or by default!

- **www.publicradiofan.com**
  This website lists all the international public radio stations, telling you which ones are currently online and giving live access.

- **http://web.ku.edu/idea**
  IDEA – the International Dialects of English Archive – is a Kansas University project; it is not, however, limited to American accents. We like it because it often offers more than one example and gives details of the gender, age, race and profession of the speakers. Each speaker reads a passage of text specifically written to contain all the possible sound combinations of English, as well as contributing some 'free conversational speech'.

Rhoticity Maps

UK and Ireland

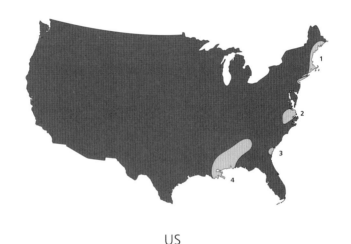

US

■ Rhotic accents   ░ Non-rhotic accents

UK and Ireland: Ireland and Scotland are wholly rhotic; England and Wales are non-rhotic, except for the South West and much of the Welsh-English border (1); areas of Pembrokeshire (2); and Central Lancashire (3).

US: This is more complex. Non-rhotic accents can traditionally be found in: the North East coast (including New York City and Boston) (1); areas of Virginia and North Carolina (2); parts of Georgia (including Savannah) (3); parts of Alabama, Mississippi and Louisiana (including New Orleans) (4). Non-rhoticity is more widespread within African-American accents.

The Vowel Spectrum

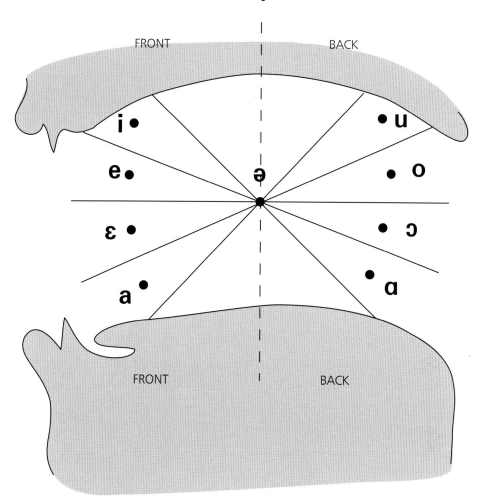

Space Exploration

The aim of this section is to take your tongue into places it may never have been before and to give your tongue and ear new reference points.

We have put *all* the extreme vowels on TRACK 82. Each vowel sound is repeated three times, followed by a short bleeping sound. After each bleep you will hear the next vowel sound.

> As you move through these shapes and sounds some of them may be familiar. It may be that they are similar to vowels from your own accent. On the other hand you may find them all very odd. Think how many new sounds you will be shaping and hearing and the flexibility you will be developing as you explore!

Be specific with the movements and sounds: your speech muscles and your ear will get some things effortlessly whilst other shapes and sounds may take more focus and practice. Your brain may try to make shortcuts by using sounds and shapes it is familiar with.

Remember, this is about exploring *new* territory!

And don't panic! If you don't get it straight away, just keep listening, playing and exploring.

Mapping your mouth: the FRONT

Preparation:

- Start with the jaw and tongue relaxed.
- The teeth should be a little apart with the tip of the tongue resting gently against the bottom front teeth.
- This places the tongue hump in the centre point of the map.
- The sound that goes with this is a small 'uh', called **neutral schwa**.

Exploration:

For each of the vowel shapes be sure to go through the following steps.

Feel It: Read the instructions/descriptions of the shape and make the shape yourself, feeling the tongue move from neutral schwa and into the vowel shape.

See It:

- Close your eyes and create a mind's eye picture of the shape you are making.

- Look at it in the mirror.

- Connect the way the shape looks and feels with the illustrations.

Hear It: Breathe out through the shape on a whisper hearing the sound the shape makes.

Add Voice: When you can **feel it**, **hear it** and **see it**, fix the point in your *muscle memory* and *add voice* to it so that you can hear it fully, keeping the shape fixed and steady.

Hear It and Compare It: Compare your sound to the sound on the CD. If it doesn't sound the same, go back through the steps, adjust things as necessary, until the sound matches.

TOP TIP

*To do accents well, you need to train your mouth and ear to **feel** and **hear** how even subtle changes in the position of the lips and tongue can affect the sounds coming out of your mouth.*

Extreme Vowel One: i

For the first extreme vowel the hump in the tongue is at its highest and furthest forward in the mouth and the lips are very spread and the jaw is close together. The resonance this shape creates is very high frequency.

See It and Feel It

- **JAW:** Let your jaw open *just a little*.
- **LIPS**: Spread the lips.
- **TONGUE**: Keep the tip of your tongue down behind your bottom teeth. Squeeze the hump of your tongue up and forwards from the centre point and towards the roof of the mouth and the gum-ridge.

Follow the instructions in the shaded boxes on pages 212–13 and focus the sound onto the gum-ridge.

Hear It [TRACK 82]

- Listen to us make the sound on the CD three times.
  (Remember, after the bleep you will hear a new vowel sound.)
- The sound has an EE-like quality.
- This is your first extreme reference point.

Extreme Vowel Two: e

If you open the jaw just the tiniest bit from the first extreme position, keeping the tongue humping up and forward, and relaxing the lips just a little, you will find yourself making extreme vowel two! It sounds a little like the Scottish vowel in TAKE and the French vowel in THÉ (tea).

See It and Feel It

- **JAW**: Let the jaw open *one finger's drop*.
- **LIPS**: Keep the lips spread.

- **TONGUE**: Keep the tip of the tongue down behind your bottom teeth. Squeeze the hump of the tongue up towards the roof of your mouth and the gum-ridge, without closing the jaw.

Follow the instructions in the shaded boxes on pages 212–13 and focus the sound on the front of your tongue.

Hear It [TRACK 82]

- Listen to us make the sound on the CD.
- The sound has an EH-like quality.
- This is your second extreme reference point.

Extreme Vowel Three: ɛ

If you open the jaw a little more, keep the tongue humped up and forward you will find yourself making extreme vowel three.

See It and Feel It

- **JAW:** Let the jaw drop open *one and a half fingers' drop*.
- **LIPS:** Keep the lips spread just a little.
- **TONGUE**: Raise the hump of the tongue just a little towards the roof of your mouth and your gum-ridge, keeping the jaw open.

Follow the instructions in the shaded boxes on pages 212–13 and focus the sound on the front of your tongue

Hear It [TRACK 82]

- Listen to us make the sound on the CD.
- The sound has an EH-like quality.
- This is your third extreme reference point.

Extreme Vowel Four: a

For the last extreme reference point at the front of your mouth the jaw is fully open. The hump in the tongue is still towards the front and fairly low in the mouth. The lips are spread a tiny bit.

See It and Feel It

- **JAW**: Let your jaw drop fully open, around *two fingers' drop.*
- **LIPS**: Keep the lips slightly spead.
- **TONGUE**: Keep the tip of your tongue forward, resting against your bottom teeth and roll the body of the tongue gently up and forward *just a little* as if letting someone glimpse your tongue piercing!

Follow the instructions in the shaded boxes on pages 212–13 and focus the sound on the front of the tongue.

Hear It [TRACK 82]
- Listen to us make the sound on the CD.
- The sound has an A-like quality.
- That is your fourth extreme reference point.

… You're halfway there, but before you go on…

Hear It [TRACK 83]
- By gliding from the top to the bottom and back again: **i̶ e̶ ɛ̶ a̶**, **a̶ ɛ̶ e̶ i̶**, passing through each of these points, you can hear and feel the rainbow of vowel possibilities at the front of your mouth.
- By adding lip-rounding to each of these tongue positions you will hear even more vowel possibilities! When you add lip-rounding to the **e** you can hear the French vowel in 'œuf', and when you round the **i** you will hear the Scots vowel in 'you'!

HOW TO DO ACCENTS

Mapping your mouth: the BACK

Preparation:

- Start with the jaw and tongue relaxed.
- The teeth should be a little apart with the tip of the tongue resting gently against the bottom front teeth.
- This places the tongue hump in the centre point of the map.
- The sound that goes with this is a small 'uh'.

Five stages of exploration:

For each of the vowel shapes be sure to go through the following steps.

Feel It: Read the instructions/descriptions of the shape and make the shape yourself, feeling the tongue move from the centre point and into the vowel shape.

See It: Close your eyes and create a mind's eye picture of the shape you are making. Look at it in the mirror.

Connect the way the shape looks and feels with the illustration.

Hear It: Breathe out through the shape on a whisper hearing the sound the shape makes.

Add Voice: When you can **feel it**, **hear it** and **see it**, fix the point in your *muscle memory* and *add voice* to it so that you can hear it fully keeping the shape fixed and steady.

Hear It and compare it: Compare your sound to the sound on the CD. If it doesn't sound the same, go back through the steps, adjust things as necessary, until the sound matches.

Extreme Vowel Five: ɑ

For the fifth extreme vowel the lips are now completely relaxed, the jaw is fully open and the hump in the tongue has moved to the back of the mouth.

See It and Feel It

- **JAW:** Let your jaw drop fully open, around *two fingers' drop*.
- **LIPS:** Keep your lips soft (not spread!)

- **TONGUE:** Anchor the tip of your tongue gently behind your bottom teeth. Relax the front of your tongue. (Yawn ever so slightly to lift the soft palate.)

Follow the instructions in the shaded box on page 217 and focus the sound on the back of the tongue.

Hear It [TRACK 84]

- Listen to us make the sound on the CD.
- The sound has an AH-like quality.
- This is your fifth extreme reference point.

Extreme Vowel Six: ɔ

For the sixth extreme vowel the lip-rounding begins!

See It and Feel It

- **JAW**: Keep the jaw almost fully open, around *one and a half fingers' drop*.
- **LIPS**: Round the lips as in the illustration.

- **TONGUE**: Keep the tip of the tongue relaxed by the bottom front teeth. The back of the tongue rises towards the soft palate. (Yawn a little to lift the soft palate out of the way!)

Follow the instructions in the shaded box on page 217 and focus the sound on the back of the tongue.

HOW TO DO ACCENTS

- Listen to us make the sound on the CD.
- The sound has a quality like the vowel in OR.
- This is your sixth extreme reference point. *(Two more to go!)*

Extreme Vowel Seven: o

We're coming into the home straight now! For this extreme vowel the jaw closes a little and the lips round even more.

See It and Feel It

- **JAW**: Close the jaw to *one finger's drop.*
- **LIPS:** Round the lips leaving enough space for one finger.

- **TONGUE**: Keep the tip of the tongue relaxed by the bottom front teeth and raise the back of the tongue towards the soft palate.

Follow the instructions in the shaded box on page 217 and focus the sound on the back of the tongue.

Hear It [TRACK 84]

- Listen to us make this sound on the CD.
- The sound has an OH-like quality.
- This is your seventh extreme reference point. *(One more to go!)*

Extreme Vowel Eight: u

This is it, the final extreme vowel. For this one the lips are fully rounded and the back of the tongue is at its highest point in the mouth making a very low resonant frequency.

See It and Feel It

- **JAW**: Let the jaw drop open *just a little*.
- **LIPS**: Pull in the cheeks and round the lips as in the illustration.

- **TONGUE**: Keep the tip of the tongue down and raise the back of your tongue as close as possible to a G position without actually making a G!

Follow the instructions in the shaded box on page 217 and focus the sound on the back of the tongue.

Hear It [TRACK 84]

- Listen to us make the sound on the CD.
- The sound has an OO-like quality.
- That is your eighth and final extreme vowel!

… But before you make yourself a cuppa…

Hear It [TRACK 85]

- By gliding from the bottom to the top and back again: ɑ‑o‑ɔ‑u, u‑ɔ‑o‑ɑ, passing through each of these points, you can hear and feel the rainbow of vowel possibilities at the back of your mouth.
- You can even glide from front to back at the top: i‑u
- And front to back at the bottom: a‑ɑ
- By adding and removing lip-rounding to each of these shapes you will hear even more possibilities!

Doing these explorations regularly will give your speech muscles and your ear the flexibility they need to be really good at accents.

Recommended Reading

Voice and Speech books

Cicely Berry, *Voice and the Actor* (John Wiley and Sons, 1991)

Barbara Houseman, *Finding Your Voice* (Nick Hern Books, 2002)

Malcolm Morrison, *Clear Speech* (A & C Black, 2001)

Michael McCallion, *The Voice Book* (Faber & Faber, 1998)

Phonetics and Phonology books

Patricia Ashby, *Speech Sounds* (Routledge, 2005)

Beverley Collins and Inger Mees, *Practical Phonetics and Phonology* (Routledge, 2003)

J C Wells, *English Intonation: An Introduction* (Cambridge University Press, 2006)

Accent books

Arthur Hughes, Peter Trudgill and Dominic Watt, *English Accents and Dialects* (Hodder Arnold, 2005)

Robert McCrum, William Cran and Robert MacNeil, *The Story of English* (Faber & Faber, 2002)

Melvyn Bragg, *The Adventure of English: The Biography of a Language* (Hodder & Stoughton, 2003)

J C Wells, *Accents of English* (three volumes; Cambridge University Press, 1982)

CD Track Listings by Chapter

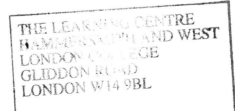
HOW TO DO ACCENTS